Sue Cunningham   Jean Cates

Appreciation

Our thanks to Justin Wells, who first suggested the cookbook. A neat idea! Especially when he offered his talent as a Western Artist for the illustrations.

We especially appreciated the double duty our families did while we were occupied with the recipes.

Ken and Peggy deserve special honors for their work before and after a cooking and also to our dad who inspired this cookbook.

A special thanks to John R. Frantz, II of Hartley, Texas for the cover photo.

About the Authors

Sue Cunningham and Jean Cates are the daughters of the late Dick and Virginia Shepherd. They were born in Turkey, Texas. Sue was born on September 8, 1934 and Jean was born on January 25, 1938. They have three older brothers, Clyde Shepherd of Nara Visa, New Mexico, Red Shepherd of Crowell, Texas, and Frank Shepherd of Channing, Texas.

In 1944 the family moved to Channing, Texas where Dick bought a place and farmed and ranched. Later, he bought a caterpillar and built tanks and did dirt work for the Matador Ranch and other ranches. He cowboyed for different ranches and would fill in as a chuckwagon cook when the cooks would get mad and quit. That is when he got interested in chuckwagon cooking. Later, he built a wagon of his own.

Sue lives in Hartley, Texas and is married to Ken Cunningham and has a daughter, Peggy Pippin, living at home. She has a step-daughter, Patsy Segedy, living in Amarillo, Texas. Patsy is married to Johnny Segedy and they have a daughter, Jamie, and a son, Scott. His wife is Brandi and their son, John Tyler. Ken works for the Soil Conservation Service of Hartley. Sue worked for the Agricultural Stabilization Conservation Service for 24½ years. She is a substitute cook at Hartley School.

Jean lives in Amarillo, Texas and is married to Wayne Cates. They have two sons, Rusty and Curtis of Amarillo. Curtis is married to Linette and they have a son, Wade Ryan. Jean and Wayne own and operate a saddle shop and make custom made saddles and tack. Jean does all the hand stamping and also works for the AAA Auto Club in Amarillo.

Both Sue and Jean stay busy during the summer going to chuck-wagon cook-off's or catering chuckwagon meals with their cooking team on weekends. They use the old chuckwagon that their dad put together and used, a family tradition.

Some of their recipes in this cookbook have been in the family for years. They have forgotten where some came from, created some, and got some from sharing with friends. So, to save face, they are only going to credit their parents, grandparents, and aunts.

Sue

About the Artist

Justin Wells of Amarillo, Texas likes to do one thing — draw horses. More specifically, he draws the people, animals, and landscapes associated with the horse culture of the American West.

Justin has exhibited his work in galleries and museums in Texas, Oklahoma, New Mexico, Colorado, Wyoming, California, and Arizona; and he has contributed illustrations for Western history magazines including "The Westerner" and the "Western Horseman." A wood-cut titled "Chuckwagon" was featured in John Meigs' **THE COWBOY IN AMERICAN PRINTS.**

Although historical illustration is a fascinating field for an artist to explore, Justin is even more interested in the Western culture as it exists today. "Cattle people are still a unique class of human being," says the artist. "They are distinctly recognizable apart from any other group of men who make their living outdoors."

It is these people and the culture that surrounds them that Justin is trying to capture on canvas and paper. He knows what he's talking about because he comes from this culture and is still very much in the middle of it. He frequently lends a hand to area cowmen at branding and round-up time.

Always an admirer of good horses, Justin raises and trains registered Quarter Horses. Next to painting a picture of a good colt, he would rather train one, and indeed one helps the other. "Knowing how a horse operates by personal experience rather than by observation enables the artist's imagination to communicate the reality of a scene much more effectively."

This is the basis of Justin's philosophy of art — one should paint what one knows and has experienced — and Justin Wells certainly knows and has experienced what he paints — The American West.

Born in Elk City, Oklahoma, Justin was raised in Oklahoma, Texas and California. His current home and studio are in Amarillo, Texas where he was recently inducted into the Texas Cowboy Artist Association.

Published and Printed By
Cookbook Publishers, Inc.
P.O. Box 15920
Lenexa, Kansas 66285-5920

THIS BOOK includes the finest plastic ring binders available, BUT, like most plastics, the BINDERS CAN BE DAMAGED BY EXCESSIVE HEAT, so AVOID exposing them to the direct rays of the SUN, or excessive heat such as IN A CAR on a hot day, or on the top of the kitchen STOVE. If not exposed to heat, the binders will last indefinitely.

1st printing   Nov. 1994   1000 books
2nd printing   March 1995   1000 books

TABLE OF CONTENTS

FAVORITE RECIPES
FROM MY COOKBOOK

Recipe Name	Page Number

Appetizers,

Beverages

Justin Wells
94
Ca ©

FOOD QUANTITIES FOR 25, 50, AND 100 SERVINGS

FOOD	25 SERVINGS	50 SERVINGS	100 SERVINGS
Rolls	4 doz.	8 doz.	16 doz.
Bread	50 slices or 3 1-lb. loaves	100 slices or 6 1-lb. loaves	200 slices or 12 1-lb. loaves
Butter	½ lb.	¾ to 1 lb.	1½ lb.
Mayonnaise	1 c.	2 to 3 c.	4 to 6 c.
Mixed filling for sandwiches (meat, eggs, fish)	1½ qt.	2½ to 3 qt.	5 to 6 qt.
Mixed filling (sweet-fruit)	1 qt.	1¾ to 2 qt.	2½ to 4 qt.
Jams & preserves	1½ lb.	3 lb.	6 lb.
Crackers	1½ lb.	3 lb.	6 lb.
Cheese (2 oz. per serving)	3 lb.	6 lb.	12 lb.
Soup	1½ gal.	3 gal.	6 gal.
Salad dressings	1 pt.	2½ pt.	½ gal.
Meat, Poultry, or Fish:			
Wieners (beef)	6½ lb.	13 lb.	25 lb.
Hamburger	9 lb.	18 lb.	35 lb.
Turkey or chicken	13 lb.	25 to 35 lb.	50 to 75 lb.
Fish, large whole (round)	13 lb.	25 lb.	50 lb.
Fish, fillets or steaks	7½ lb.	15 lb.	30 lb.
Salads, Casseroles, Vegetables:			
Potato salad	4¼ qt.	2¼ gal.	4½ gal.
Scalloped potatoes	4½ qt. or 1 12x20" pan	8½ qt.	17 qt.
Mashed potatoes	9 lb.	18-20 lb.	25-35 lb.
Spaghetti	1¼ gal.	2½ gal.	5 gal.
Baked beans	¾ gal.	1¼ gal.	2½ gal.
Jello salad	¾ gal.	1¼ gal.	2½ gal.
Canned vegetables	1 #10 can	2½ #10 cans	4 #10 cans
Fresh Vegetables:			
Lettuce (for salads)	4 heads	8 heads	15 heads
Carrots (3 oz. or ½ c.)	6¼ lb.	12½ lb.	25 lb.
Tomatoes	3-5 lb.	7-10 lb.	14-20 lb.
Desserts:			
Watermelon	37½ lb.	75 lb.	150 lb.
Fruit cup (½ c. per serving)	3 qt.	6 qt.	12 qt.
Cake	1 10x12" sheet cake 1½ 10" layer cakes	1 12x20" sheet cake 3 10" layer cakes	2 12x20" sheet cakes 6 10" layer cakes
Whipping cream	¾ pt.	1½ to 2 pt.	3 pt.
Ice Cream:			
Brick	3¼ qt.	6½ qt.	12½ qt.
Bulk	2¼ qt.	4½ qt. or 1¼ gal.	9 qt. or 2½ gal.
Beverages:			
Coffee	½ lb. and 1½ gal. water	1 lb. and 3 gal. water	2 lb. and 6 gal. water
Tea	1/12 lb. and 1½ gal. water	⅙ lb. and 3 gal. water	⅓ lb. and 6 gal. water
Lemonade	10 to 15 lemons, 1½ gal. water	20 to 30 lemons, 3 gal. water	40 to 60 lemons, 6 gal. water

APPETIZERS, BEVERAGES

HISTORY OF THE CHUCKWAGON

Dick Shepherd (1904-1984), cowboy/rancher of the Texas Panhandle and North Eastern New Mexico, worked the large ranches of the area which included the Matador Ranch, both upper and lower divisions. When the Matadors sold out in the early 50's, Dick was given the chuckwagon from the Alamositas Division to use. He cooked for fall and spring round-ups on many of the ranches that he had cowboyed for in his earlier years.

Dick lost possession of the original wagon, so he acquired an XIT Ranch Wagon and put his chuck box and other equipment on it and kept on cooking. This chuckwagon was kept to a near likeness of the Matador chuckwagon. Unique features of the Matador chuckwagon are things like no spring seat (sat on bedrolls), front commissary box (feed box for horse and mule feed), and they ordered metal tongues when they became available.

Dick never thought about showing off this old wagon as it was cobbled together for use. Any modernization that could be done or afforded was done. This family heirloom has been untouched since Dick passed away and will not be modernized nor authenticated as long as the Shepherd family owns it. There is XIT Ranch history, Matador Ranch history, and Dick Shepherd history in this wagon.

Sue Cunninghan, Jean Cates, and Clyde Shepherd (three of Shepherd's kids) own and use this wagon regularly. Headquarters for this wagon is Hartley, Texas, located in the Texas Panhandle in Hartley County. This wagon is often used by photographers, artists, and writers to document history and western heritage. It is used on special occasions such as chuckwagon cook-off's and catering services. In April of 1993 this wagon was featured on the Texas Country Reporter TV program and in August of 1994 it was featured on PBS Channel 2 TV program.

Each year the family uses the wagon to cook for the Matador cowboys at the Matador Cowboy Reunion held on the third weekend of August each year in Channing, Texas. The old Matador hands feel that this is their wagon.

Sue, edited by Jean

CHEESE LOG

2 lb. Velveeta cheese
1 (8 oz.) pkg. cream cheese
½ lb. Longhorn cheese

1 Tbsp. garlic salt
1 small grated onion
1 c. finely chopped pecans

Grate cheese. Combine other ingredients; roll into logs. Sprinkle chili powder and red pepper (cayenne) on waxed paper. Put cheese logs onto waxed paper; roll up, then chill. Serve on Ritz crackers. Slice ¼ inch thick.

CHILI CON QUESO DIP

1 c. chopped onion
2 cloves garlic, chopped
¼ c. cooking oil
3 to 4 c. canned tomatoes
1 small can chopped green chilies
¼ c. finely chopped bell pepper

¼ tsp. salt
Pepper to taste
½ c. half & half cream
2 c. sharp Cheddar, grated
1 tsp. Worcestershire sauce

Saute onions in oil until golden. Add garlic; cook slightly. Chop canned tomatoes into small pieces and add with canned green chilies, fresh pepper, salt, and pepper. Cook for 5 minutes. Add half & half, grated Cheddar, and Worcestershire sauce; stir until cheese is melted. Keep in warm container over hot water or on a warming tray and serve hot with crackers or tortilla chips.

CHEX PARTY MIX

½ c. butter
½ c. Worcestershire sauce
1¼ tsp. seasoned salt
2 c. Wheat Chex

3 c. Rice Chex
3 c. Corn Chex
1 to 2 c. salted nuts
1 c. pretzels

Melt butter. Add Worcestershire sauce and seasoned salt; mix well. Gradually add Chex cereal and nuts. Make sure you mix well. Heat at 250° for 1 hour. Mix every 15 minutes.

Can be put in a brown paper sack and cooked in microwave for 15 to 20 minutes. When using the conventional method, use a roaster pan to cook it in.

FRUIT DIP

1 (8 oz.) softened cream cheese

1 (7½ oz.) jar marshmallow cream

Whip together cream cheese and marshmallow cream. Serve with a variety of fruits that will dip (apples, strawberries, peaches, pineapple chunks, etc.).

GREEN CHILI DIP

1 (8 oz.) pkg. cream cheese
½ c. sour cream
½ c. salad dressing

1 (4 oz.) can chopped green chilies
4 Tbsp. minced onion
Dash of salt

Mix all ingredients in order given. Chill overnight. Serve with corn chips or crackers.

GUACAMOLE DIP

1 large avocado, peeled, seeded, and mashed
2 Tbsp. picante sauce
¼ c. chopped onion

1 tsp. lemon juice
¼ tsp. salt
1 tomato, diced
Garlic salt

Combine all ingredients; mix well. Makes about 1 cup.

HOT CHEESE AND SAUSAGE DIP

2 lb. Velveeta cheese, melted
1 lb. "hot" sausage
1 pkg. Good Seasons garlic salad dressing mix

1 large can evaporated milk

Cook sausage; drain and crumble. Add remaining ingredients, mixing well, and serve with Doritos or tostados.

MICROWAVE CARAMEL CORN

1 c. brown sugar
¼ c. white Karo syrup
½ c. oleo

½ tsp. salt
½ tsp. baking soda
3 to 4 qt. popped corn

Bring to boil in microwave; boil for 2 minutes. Remove and add ½ teaspoon baking soda and stir. Pour 3 to 4 quarts popped corn into clean grocery bag. Pour caramel mixture over corn and close bag top securely. Shake bag vigorously. Cook in bag in microwave 1½ minutes. Remove and shake. Cook another 1½ minutes. (May need cooked longer, depending on weather.) Pour into pan and allow to cool.

ONION SOUP DIP

1 env. onion soup mix
1 pt. sour cream

1 medium tomato, chopped
1 small green pepper, diced

Blend soup with sour cream. Add remaining ingredients. Chill at least 1 hour. Makes 2½ cups. Serve with assorted chips.

POPCORN BALLS

1 c. sugar
⅓ c. white corn syrup
⅓ c. water
¼ c. butter

¾ tsp. vanilla
¾ tsp. salt
3 qt. popped corn

Keep popped corn in oven at 300°F. Stir and cook sugar, water, corn syrup, butter, and salt. Boil until drops dropped into cup of cold water are at brittle stage. Add vanilla. Pour over popped corn; stir. Grease hands with butter and shape into balls. Can add nuts and cherries, etc. if desired.

RANCH DIP

2 tsp. instant minced onion
½ tsp. salt
⅛ tsp. garlic powder

1 Tbsp. parsley flakes
1 c. mayonnaise
1 c. sour cream

Combine dry ingredients. Stir in mayonnaise and sour cream. Chill before serving. Makes 2 cups.

For Ranch Dressing: Use 1 cup buttermilk in place of the sour cream.

SALMON BALL

1 (16 oz.) can salmon
1 (8 oz.) pkg. cream cheese
2 Tbsp. freshly squeezed lemon
   juice
3 tsp. grated onion
2 tsp. horseradish

½ tsp. salt
Dash of Worcestershire sauce
Several dashes cayenne pepper
½ tsp. liquid smoke
½ c. chopped pecans
3 Tbsp. minced fresh parsley

Drain salmon; remove skin and bones, then flake with fork. In small bowl of electric mixer, cream cheese and blend in lemon juice, onion, horseradish, salt, Worcestershire sauce, cayenne pepper, and liquid smoke. When well blended, stir in salmon. Check seasonings; it might need a little more salt.

Combine pecans and parsley; spread on a sheet of waxed paper. Turn salmon out onto this mixture and turn it this way and that until all sides of the mound are coated. Wrap in waxed paper and chill thoroughly before using.

THE MULE MAN

Our Daddy loved working horses and mules. He, like anyone else his age, grew up working them on the family farm and ranch.

In 1939 Daddy and some other men took a stage coach from Mineral Wells, Texas to New York City to the New York Worlds Fair. He used some of his paint horses to pull the stage coach. Polecat and Pathfinder could be worked to pull anything but could not be ridden with a saddle. After we moved to Channing, Daddy had a bucking string of horses. He also bucked those paint horses.

Daddy had mules off and on ever since I could remember, but got serious about trading mules about the time he started using the Matador chuckwagon to cook at round-up time on area ranches. He also traded a lot of harness. Lots of people just knew him as "The Mule Man."

He had this special mule called Jenny Bars. He took her to the Mule-O-Rama in Ruidoso, New Mexico. Our sons, Curtis and Rusty Cates, gave Jenny Bars a bath, clipped her ears, and the whole works. Curtis showed her at halter. Bobby Chambers rode her in the Western Pleasure Class.

Daddy had a way with mules. He could just drive out in the pasture, catch the mules, and load them in the trailer without even penning them up.

Jean, edited by Sue

SAUSAGE BALLS

1 lb. hot bulk sausage
2 c. shredded Cheddar cheese

2 c. biscuit mix
1 Tbsp. poultry seasoning

Combine all ingredients, mixing well. Roll into walnut-size balls. Place on an ungreased baking sheet and bake at 400° for 15 minutes. Drain on paper towels. Serve hot. Makes about 48.

TACO DIP

1 lb. Velveeta cheese
1 can Ro-Tel tomatoes

1 lb. hamburger
1 pkg. taco seasoning

Melt cheese in a double boiler with the juice from the Ro-Tel tomatoes. Chop tomatoes very finely and add to cheese. Let simmer ½ hour. Cook hamburger until brown; drain excess grease. Add ¾ cup water and ½ package taco seasoning. Let simmer for ½ hour. Add hamburger to cheese and let simmer for 1 hour, stirring occasionally. Can be used as a dip for Doritos or topping for burritos or tacos.

TEXAS CAVIAR

2 cans black-eyed peas, drained
   and rinsed
1 pkg. Italian dressing, by direction
   (or 1 c.)
1 bunch chopped green onion or 1
   small chopped onion

1 medium or 2 small green peppers
   (red or green)
4 oz. can diced jalapeno peppers
   (5 fresh or ½ c.)
4 oz. can diced green chiles
½ tsp. garlic salt

Mix all ingredients and chill. Serve with Doritos or Fritos.

TEX-MEX DIP

1 can bean dip
3 ripe avocados, mashed
2 tsp. lemon juice
1/4 tsp. pepper
3/4 tsp. salt
1 c. sour cream

1/2 c. mayonnaise
1 pkg. taco seasoning mix
1/2 c. chopped onion
1 or 2 chopped tomatoes
1 or 2 c. shredded cheese
1/2 c. chopped or sliced olives

Layer 1: Bean dip.

Layer 2: Combine avocados, lemon juice, salt, and pepper.

Layer 3: Combine sour cream, mayonnaise, and taco seasoning.

Layer 4: Add onion.

Layer 5: Add tomatoes.

Layer 6: Add shredded cheese.

Layer 7: Add olives.

Serve at room temperature or chilled.

SPINACH DIP

1 env. Lipton vegetable soup mix
1 (16 oz.) ctn. sour cream
1/2 c. mayonnaise
1 (10 oz.) pkg. frozen chopped
    spinach, thawed and squeezed
    dry

1 (8 oz.) can water chestnuts
1 bunch green onions, chopped

In medium bowl, blend soup mix with sour cream and mayonnaise. Mix in spinach, water chestnuts, and green onion. Chill at least 2 hours before serving. (It is good with 2 packages of the soup mix instead of 1.) Makes about 3 1/2 to 4 cups.

BANANA SLUSH PUNCH

8 bananas
2 large cans pineapple juice
2 (12 oz.) cans frozen orange juice

2 cans water
2 c. sugar
1 to 2 qt. 7-Up

Put bananas in blender and mash. Add and mix well the pineapple juice, orange juice, water, and sugar. Freeze. Remove from freezer a few hours before serving, until it thaws to a slushy state. Add 1 to 2 quarts of 7-Up.

BREAKFAST COCOA

5 to 6 Tbsp. cocoa
4 to 6 Tbsp. sugar
Dash of salt

½ c. water
3½ c. milk

Mix cocoa, sugar, and salt with water; cook, while stirring, for 3 minutes. Stir in milk and heat to boiling point but *do not boil.* Beat with rotary beater just before serving. Top with marshmallows or vanilla ice cream.

EGGNOG

8 whole eggs
1½ c. sugar

½ gal. vanilla ice cream
1 tsp. nutmeg

Beat eggs until light and fluffy, then add sugar and ice cream. Add enough milk to make 1 gallon. Add nutmeg. Let ice cream soften until it will blend with mixer into eggs. (Sorry - no spirits included.)

HOT CHOCOLATE MIX

2 lb. box Nestle Quik
1 (8 qt.) box powdered milk
16 oz. jar Coffee-mate

1 lb. powdered sugar
½ tsp. salt
3 Tbsp. cocoa

Mix all together. Use 2 to 3 heaping tablespoons to a cup of hot water. Store in a tight sealed container.

INSTANT SPICED TEA

2 c. instant Tang (or 18 oz.)
2⅓ c. sugar
1 pkg. instant lemonade mix

1½ c. instant tea
2 tsp. ground cloves
2 tsp. ground cinnamon

Mix well and store in a tightly closed container. To serve, put 2 to 3 teaspoons to a cup of boiling water.

JELL-O BASE PUNCH

3 (3 oz.) pkg. Jell-O
1 pkg. Kool-Aid
3 c. sugar
4 c. boiling water

2 qt. ginger ale
2 (6 oz.) cans frozen orange juice
1 (6 oz.) can frozen lemon juice
1 gal. cold water

Dissolve Jell-O, Kool-Aid, and sugar in boiling water. Add juices and cold water. Cool and add ginger ale. Makes 50 servings.

PARTY PUNCH

1 (12 oz.) frozen lemonade
1 (12 oz.) frozen orange juice
1 (12 oz.) frozen pineapple juice

1 (46 oz.) Hawaiian Punch
1 large ginger ale

Combine all ingredients. Mix and serve over ice.

Notes

Soups,
Salads

A HANDY SPICE AND HERB GUIDE

ALLSPICE-a pea-sized fruit that grows in Mexico, Jamaica, Central and South America. Its delicate flavor resembles a blend of cloves, cinnamon, and nutmeg. USES: (Whole) Pickles, meats, boiled fish, gravies; (Ground) Puddings, relishes, fruit preserves, baking.

BASIL-the dried leaves and stems of an herb grown in the United States and North Mediterranean area. Has an aromatic, leafy flavor. USES: For flavoring tomato dishes and tomato paste, turtle soup; also use in cooked peas, squash, snap beans; sprinkle chopped over lamb chops and poultry.

BAY LEAVES-the dried leaves of an evergreen grown in the eastern Mediterranean countries. Has a sweet, herbaceous floral spice note. USES: For pickling, stews, for spicing sauces and soup. Also use with a variety of meats and fish.

CARAWAY-the seed of a plant grown in the Netherlands. Flavor that combines the tastes of anise and dill. USES: For the cordial Kummel, baking breads; often added to sauerkraut, noodles, cheese spreads. Also adds zest to French fried potatoes, liver, canned asparagus.

CURRY POWDER-a ground blend of ginger, turmeric, fenugreek seed, as many as 16 to 20 spices. USES: For all Indian curry recipes such as lamb, chicken, and rice, eggs, vegetables, and curry puffs.

DILL-the small, dark seed of the dill plant grown in India, having a clean, aromatic taste. USES: Dill is a predominant seasoning in pickling recipes; also adds pleasing flavor to sauerkraut, potato salad, cooked macaroni, and green apple pie.

MACE-the dried covering around the nutmeg seed. Its flavor is similar to nutmeg, but with a fragrant, delicate difference. USES: (Whole) For pickling, fish, fish sauce, stewed fruit. (Ground) Delicious in baked goods, pastries, and doughnuts, adds unusual flavor to chocolate desserts.

MARJORAM-an herb of the mint family, grown in France and Chile. Has a minty-sweet flavor. USES: In beverages, jellies, and to flavor soups, stews, fish, sauces. Also excellent to sprinkle on lamb while roasting.

MSG (MONOSODIUM GLUTAMATE)-a vegetable protein derivative for raising the effectiveness of natural food flavors. USES: Small amounts, adjusted to individual taste, can be added to steaks, roasts, chops, seafoods, stews, soups, chowder, chop suey, and cooked vegetables.

OREGANO-a plant of the mint family and a species of marjoram of which the dried leaves are used to make an herb seasoning. USES: An excellent flavoring for any tomato dish, especially pizza, chili con carne, and Italian specialties.

PAPRIKA-a mild, sweet red pepper growing in Spain, Central Europe, and the United States. Slightly aromatic and prized for brilliant red color. USES: A colorful garnish for pale foods, and for seasoning Chicken Paprika, Hungarian Goulash, salad dressings.

POPPY-the seed of a flower grown in Holland. Has a rich fragrance and crunchy, nut-like flavor. USES: Excellent as a topping for breads, rolls, and cookies. Also delicious in buttered noodles.

ROSEMARY-an herb (like a curved pine needle) grown in France, Spain, and Portugal, and having a sweet fresh taste. USES: In lamb dishes, in soups, stews, and to sprinkle on beef before roasting.

SAGE-the leaf of a shrub grown in Greece, Yugoslavia, and Albania. Flavor is camphoraceous and minty. USES: For meat and poultry stuffing, sausages, meat loaf, hamburgers, stews, and salads.

THYME-the leaves and stems of a shrub grown in France and Spain. Has a strong, distinctive flavor. USES: For poultry seasoning, croquettes, fricassees, and fish dishes. Also tasty on fresh sliced tomatoes.

TURMERIC-a root of the ginger family, grown in India, Haiti, Jamaica, and Peru, having a mild, ginger-pepper flavor. USES: As a flavoring and coloring in prepared mustard and in combination with mustard as a flavoring for meats, dressings, salads.

SOUPS, SALADS

SETTING UP CAMP

We use a flat bed trailer designed especially for hauling the chuckwagon on. It has tracks installed in the bed of the trailer for wheels of the wagon to go in. We also boom the wagon down to keep it from moving around while being hauled. It has a wench that hooks up to the battery of the pickup to use for loading and unloading the wagon.

We drive to the location set for the cooking with all the equipment we need. Unload the wagon and the wagon fly. The wagon fly is a big canvas tarp put up to cook under and for protection from rain and sun. Unroll and stretch out the wagon fly and measure where to put the stakes. Drive the stakes into the ground with a sledge hammer, it is hard work. Put up the wagon fly and stretch it tight.

Unload fire irons and measure how big to dig your fire pit. Fire irons are made to go over the fire pit to keep pots and pans from falling through. Dig the fire pit with a shovel and pick. We take turns as the ground is usually hard and dry. The fire pit should be about 5 feet long, 1 foot wide, and about 1½ feet deep. Dig another shallow hole on the side (not under the fly) to use for burning mesquite or oak wood. You might have several small holes just big enough for your Dutch ovens to set in. We use 2 or 3 kinds of wood. Old cedar post make a quick hot fire in the pit and mesquite or oak wood is good for the Dutch oven cooking. The coals last longer if hard wood is used.

Unload tables and set them up. We carry a 55 gallon barrel with a lid on it for water. Unload the water barrel and fill with water that you have carried from home in buckets, or go somewhere and get some. We carry 2 round-up trays (tubs) to wash and rinse pots and pans. We have an old cream can we carry to heat water in. We like to set up the wagon the night before the cooking. We usually leave the wagon fly up all night.

Sue, edited by Jean

CHILI BEAN SOUP

2 lb. lean ground beef
1 green pepper, chopped
1 medium onion, thinly sliced
1 clove garlic, minced
¼ c. cooking oil
2 (16 oz.) cans tomatoes
1 to 2 Tbsp. chili powder

1½ tsp. salt
½ tsp. ground oregano
½ tsp. cumin seed
3 dashes Tabasco
1 c. hot water
2 c. pinto beans, cooked

Cook beef, green pepper, onion, and garlic in oil until beef is slightly browned. Add all ingredients, except beans, and simmer, uncovered, 45 minutes. Stir in undrained pinto beans; simmer 15 minutes. For a thinner mixture, add water. Serves 8.

COTTAGE CHEESE SALAD

1 can tomato soup
1 pkg. lemon Jell-O
1 c. cottage cheese
1 c. celery
½ c. ripe olives

1 bell pepper
2 Tbsp. sugar
⅛ tsp. salt
1 c. salad dressing

Heat soup (hot). Add dry Jell-O. Stir 2 minutes to dissolve; cool. Add cottage cheese, then add chopped celery, chopped bell pepper, chopped ripe olives, sugar, salt, and last of all, add salad dressing. Serve on lettuce leaf.

NAPA (CHINESE) CABBAGE SOUP

1 head Napa cabbage
1 box (2 pkg.) Campbell's chicken
   noodle soup (with white chicken
   meat)

1 can sliced water chestnuts, cut in
   fourths

Wash and cut up Napa cabbage in large pan; cover with water and bring to boil. Cook until almost tender. Rinse, rinse, and rerinse water chestnuts. Add to cabbage. Add soup packages; simmer until noodles are done. Might need to add chicken bouillon to taste according to size of cabbage head. On serving, chop 1 green onion.

VEGETABLE BEEF SOUP

2 lb. stew meat
6 large carrots
5 medium potatoes
4 stalks celery
1 onion

Tenderizer
1 large can tomatoes
2 cans mixed (Veg-All) vegetables
1 small can tomato sauce
Salt and pepper to taste

Sprinkle cut up stew meat with tenderizer; brown in pan. Add water to cover and cook until tender. Meanwhile, in another pot, cut up peeled carrots. Let cook until almost tender. Add cut up potatoes (bite-size chunks). Add celery and onions. Cook veggies until done. Add tomatoes, cut up. Add Veg-All vegetables and tomato sauce. Drain cooked beef and add to soup. Add salt and pepper to taste. Serve hot.

ANGEL HASH SALAD

1 (No. 2) can crushed pineapple
1 (No. 2) can fruit cocktail
2 Tbsp. cornstarch
¼ c. sugar
2 egg yolks, beaten

1 c. whipped topping
¼ c. chopped nuts
2 c. miniature marshmallows
3 bananas

Drain fruit and reserve juice. Combine cornstarch and sugar in pan; mix well. Add 1 cup juice and egg yolks. Blend well and cook over heat until thick, stirring constantly. Cool. Fold in whipped topping, nuts, marshmallows, bananas, pineapple, and fruit cocktail. Cover and chill overnight.

CHERRY SALAD

1 can cherry pie filling
1 can Eagle Brand milk
1 large can crushed pineapple,
    drained

2 bananas, sliced
1 c. chopped pecans
1 (8 oz.) ctn. Cool Whip

Mix all together and place in refrigerator.

HAVEN OF DELIGHT SALAD

20 marshmallows or 1 pkg.
    miniature marshmallows
1 pkg. cream cheese

1 large can fruit cocktail
½ c. chopped nuts
1 c. whipping cream, whipped

Warm cream cheese enough to mix well. Cut large marshmallows in fourths or use miniature marshmallows. Mix with cream cheese. Drain juice from fruit cocktail. Add to cream cheese mixture. Add chopped nuts. Add whipped cream and serve.

MRS. C'S JELLO

1 pkg. apricot Jell-O
1 small can crushed pineapple

1 c. pecans
3 stalks celery

Make Jell-O as directed. Add pineapple juice and all. Add diced celery and pecan pieces. Refrigerate until set and serve.

This recipe is best with apricot Jell-O.

PISTACHIO SALAD

1 (3 oz.) pkg. pistachio pudding mix
1 (8 oz.) ctn. Cool Whip
½ c. chopped pecans

1 (20 oz.) can crushed pineapple
    (including juice)
1 small ctn. cottage cheese

Mix pudding mix and pineapple. Add a little green food coloring. Fold in cottage cheese and Cool Whip. Add pecans and chill.

WALDORF PARTY SALAD

3 c. diced apples
1 c. seedless grapes
1 c. miniature marshmallows
½ c. Miracle Whip

½ c. walnut or pecan halves,
    toasted
1 c. Cool Whip
Lettuce

Combine fruit, marshmallows, and nuts; toss lightly. Combine Cool Whip and salad dressing. Fold into fruit salad. Chill. Serve on a lettuce leaf.

THE BRAHMA'S

We moved to Channing, Texas in 1944. We soon built the Rodeo arena at our place. Calf ropers came from all over the area to rope on Sunday afternoon.

The ropers formed a roping club. Each member bought a Brahma (Bramer) heifer every year. Our bothers always kept theirs, and got a herd started.

A few years later in the early 50's Clyde was off working on a ranch. Red and Frank were in the service, during the Korean Conflict, and Daddy was off working building dirt tanks on ranches.

That left Sue and myself to take care of the cattle. Daddy would lease grazing land sometimes 15 or 20 miles away. We loved moving those Bramers. They would follow instead of having to drive them. You could really make good time with them. Not like our Daddy's white faced herefords.

We had this Bramer named Baldy. We would be moving the cattle along the fence. Baldy would jump the fence, graze a bit, then jump back over the fence and join the herd.

Jean, edited by Sue

CHEESE STUFFED BELL PEPPERS

4 large bell peppers
2 (8 oz.) pkg. cream cheese
½ c. minced onion

½ c. chopped dill pickle
½ c. chopped pecans

Hollow out and clean bell peppers from the top. Soften cream cheese and add onion, dill pickle, and pecans. Mix well and stuff bell peppers. Chill overnight. Slice and serve.

CORN SALAD

¾ c. vinegar
¾ c. corn oil
¾ c. sugar
1 tsp. salt
¼ tsp. pepper
1 c. chopped green pepper

1 c. chopped celery
¼ c. chopped green onions and
    tops
1 (16 oz.) can shoe peg corn
1 (8 oz.) can small peas
1 (2 oz.) jar pimientos, diced

Combine vinegar, oil, sugar, salt, and pepper in a saucepan; bring to a boil. Set aside to cool. Place green pepper, celery, and onions in a large bowl. Drain corn, peas, and pimientos; combine with vegetables. Pour vinegar and oil mixture over the vegetables and mix; refrigerate for several hours. Serves 8 to 10.

CORN BREAD SALAD

2 (6 oz.) pkg. corn bread mix
    (regular or Mexican)
1 medium chopped onion (or 2
    bunches green onions)
1 bell pepper, chopped

1 tomato, diced
1 pt. jar mayonnaise (or salad
    dressing)
Salt and pepper to taste

Mix corn bread mix according to directions. Cook and cool. Crumble cooled corn bread into large bowl. Add onion, bell pepper, tomato, and mayonnaise. Salt and pepper to taste.

LIMA BEAN SALAD

3 c. cooked lima beans
¼ c. chopped pimentos
½ c. chopped celery

½ c. chopped green bell pepper
½ tsp. salt

Dressing:

6 Tbsp. salad dressing
½ tsp. garlic
⅛ tsp. salt

Dash of pepper
1 Tbsp. lemon juice
1 tsp. milk

Mix beans, pimentos, celery, bell pepper, and salt together. Mix together in separate bowl the salad dressing, garlic, salt, pepper, lemon juice, and milk. Mix well and add to bean mixture. Stir and serve.

MACARONI SALAD

1 (8 oz.) pkg. macaroni
1½ c. mayonnaise
½ c. chopped celery
1 large onion, chopped

½ c. shredded carrot
¼ c. chopped green pepper
Salt
Pepper

Cook macaroni in boiling water according to package directions. Drain, rinse with cold water, and drain again. Stir in mayonnaise; chill. Add celery, onion, green pepper, carrot, and seasoning. Refrigerate. Serves 8.

MASHED POTATO SALAD

6 medium potatoes, peeled and cut
    into small pieces
1 medium onion, diced
2 boiled eggs

Diced dill pickles
Mustard
Mayonnaise
1 small jar pimentos

Peel and cut potatoes into small chunks. Boil until tender and drain; mash. Add pickles and onions. Grate peeled boiled eggs with vegetable grater; add to potatoes. Add pimentos. Mix and add mustard and mayonnaise to taste. If too dry, add small amount of dill pickle juice.

POTATO SALAD

8 medium potatoes
5 eggs, boiled
1 medium onion, chopped
3 dill pickles, chopped
1 c. Miracle Whip

¼ c. mustard
¼ c. pickle juice
1 small can pimientos
Salt to taste
Pepper to taste

Boil potatoes and eggs; refrigerate overnight. Peel potatoes and eggs; dice. Add all other ingredients and mix well. Chill and eat.

SEVEN LAYER SALAD

1 head lettuce, chopped
1 c. frozen peas, thawed
1 c. onion, diced
1 c. celery, chopped

2 c. real mayonnaise
1 c. Cheddar cheese, grated
½ c. bacon bits

Place each ingredient in layers in the above order. Looks pretty in a deep clear bowl. Chill.

TACO SALAD

1½ lb. ground beef
1½ c. diced onions
3 cloves garlic, diced
Salt to taste
Chili powder to taste
Cumin to taste

1 lb. Velveeta cheese
1 can Ro-Tel tomatoes
1 large head lettuce, coarsely
   chopped
1 large tomato, diced
1 large pkg. corn chips

Brown beef in small amount of oil. Saute onions and garlic until soft but not brown. Add to meat; simmer for a few minutes. Season with salt, chili powder, and cumin. Melt cheese in top of double boiler. Add Ro-Tel tomatoes. Place lettuce and tomatoes in large salad bowl. Add meat and vegetables. Mix lightly; top with hot cheese mixture. Sprinkle with corn chips. Serve immediately.

VEGETABLE RICE SALAD

1 c. mayonnaise
1 Tbsp. vinegar
1 small clove garlic, minced
1 tsp. salt
¼ tsp. pepper

2 c. cooked rice, cooled
1 (10 oz.) pkg. frozen peas, thawed
½ c. shredded carrot
¼ c. chopped green onion

Combine first 5 ingredients. Stir in remaining ingredients; cover and chill.

VEGETABLE SALAD

1 head cauliflower
1 bunch broccoli
1 lb. Cheddar cheese
1 can ripe olives

1 jar green olives
1 small jar pimentos
½ c. Miracle Whip
Bacon bits

Prepare cauliflower and broccoli into desired pieces. Cube cheese into small cubes. Slice olives and chop pimentos. Add Miracle Whip to vegetables and mix. Sprinkle with bacon bits. Chill.

Vegetables

EQUIVALENT CHART

3 tsp.	1 Tbsp.
2 Tbsp.	⅛ c.
4 Tbsp.	¼ c.
8 Tbsp.	½ c.
16 Tbsp.	1 c.
5 Tbsp. + 1 tsp.	⅓ c.
12 Tbsp.	¾ c.
4 oz.	½ c.
8 oz.	1 c.
16 oz.	1 lb.
1 oz.	2 Tbsp. fat or liquid
2 c.	1 pt.
2 pt.	1 qt.
1 qt.	4 c.
⅝ c.	½ c. + 2 Tbsp.
⅞ c.	¾ c. + 2 Tbsp.
1 jigger	1½ fl. oz. (3 Tbsp.)
8 to 10 egg whites	1 c.
12 to 14 egg yolks	1 c.
1 c. unwhipped cream	2 c. whipped
1 lb. shredded American cheese	4 c.
¼ lb. crumbled Bleu cheese	1 c.
1 lemon	3 Tbsp. juice
1 orange	⅓ c. juice
1 lb. unshelled walnuts	1½ to 1¾ c. shelled
2 c. fat	1 lb.
1 lb. butter	2 c. or 4 sticks
2 c. granulated sugar	1 lb.
3½-4 c. unsifted powdered sugar	1 lb.
2¼ c. packed brown sugar	1 lb.
4 c. sifted flour	1 lb.
4½ c. cake flour	1 lb.
3½ c. unsifted whole wheat flour	1 lb.
4 oz. (1 to 1¼ c.) uncooked macaroni	2¼ c. cooked
7 oz. spaghetti	4 c. cooked
4 oz. (1½ to 2 c.) uncooked noodles	2 c. cooked
28 saltine crackers	1 c. crumbs
4 slices bread	1 c. crumbs
14 square graham crackers	1 c. crumbs
22 vanilla wafers	1 c. crumbs

SUBSTITUTIONS FOR A MISSING INGREDIENT

1 square **chocolate** (1 ounce) = 3 or 4 tablespoons cocoa plus ½ tablespoon fat

1 tablespoon **cornstarch** (for thickening) = 2 tablespoons flour

1 cup sifted **all-purpose flour** = 1 cup plus 2 tablespoons sifted cake flour

1 cup sifted **cake flour** = 1 cup minus 2 tablespoons sifted all-purpose flour

1 teaspoon **baking powder** = ¼ teaspoon baking soda plus ½ teaspoon cream of tartar

1 cup **sour milk** = 1 cup sweet milk into which 1 tablespoon vinegar or lemon juice has been stirred

1 cup **sweet milk** = 1 cup sour milk or buttermilk plus ½ teaspoon baking soda

¾ cup **cracker crumbs** = 1 cup bread crumbs

1 cup **cream, sour, heavy** = ⅓ cup butter and ⅔ cup milk in any sour milk recipe

1 teaspoon **dried herbs** = 1 tablespoon fresh herbs

1 cup **whole milk** = ½ cup evaporated milk and ½ cup water or 1 cup reconstituted nonfat dry milk and 1 tablespoon butter

2 ounces **compressed yeast** = 3 (¼ ounce) packets of dry yeast

1 tablespoon **instant minced onion, rehydrated** = 1 small fresh onion

1 tablespoon **prepared mustard** = 1 teaspoon dry mustard

⅛ teaspoon **garlic powder** = 1 small pressed clove of garlic

1 lb. **whole dates** = 1½ cups, pitted and cut

3 medium **bananas** = 1 cup mashed

3 cups **dry corn flakes** = 1 cup crushed

10 **miniature marshmallows** = 1 large marshmallow

GENERAL OVEN CHART

Very slow oven	250° to 300°F.
Slow oven	300° to 325°F.
Moderate oven	325° to 375°F.
Medium hot oven	375° to 400°F.
Hot oven	400° to 450°F.
Very hot oven	450° to 500°F.

CONTENTS OF CANS

Of the different sizes of cans used by commercial canners, the most common are:

Size:	Average Contents
8 oz.	1 cup
Picnic	1¼ cups
No. 300	1¾ cups
No. 1 tall	2 cups
No. 303	2 cups
No. 2	2½ cups
No. 2½	3½ cups
No. 3	4 cups
No. 10	12 to 13 cups

VEGETABLES

THINGS TO CHECK BEFORE A COOKING

Go through the wagon to make sure you have all the pots, pans, and utensils needed for that cooking. Check foods on the wagon like flour, corn meal, sugar, beans, coffee, salt, pepper, and all the other spices, also paper goods. Order meat and pick it up when you buy the rest of the groceries. Cut up the meat and refrigerate it. Soak the beans the night before the cooking.

Load wood, 3 kinds if needed. Make sure you have the wagon fly, fly poles, stakes, sledge hammer, shovels, pick, axe, wire stretchers, tubs, water can for heating water, water barrel, trash cans, tables, chairs, gas can, gas, grocery box, lanterns, buckets to haul water in, and water hose loaded. Load bedrolls and tepees if you plan to spend the night. Most of the bedrolls stay on the wagon along with the Dutch ovens. Make sure you take slickers; you can never tell about the rain.

Sue, edited by Jean

THINGS TO DO AFTER A COOKING

Unload the pickup of things that weren't on the wagon, such as chairs, grocery box, buckets, and coolers. Empty the trash. Check all the pans you used and wash them again if they didn't get clean. Get everything cleaned up again to get ready for your next cooking. Soak and wash smoky clothes, aprons, towels, and rags. We keep 2 or 3 kinds of wood. We cut it in the size pieces we need to store in the barn to keep it dry for the next cooking.

Sometimes we have been in rain and have to dry everything out like bedrolls, wash bedding, dry out tarps, wagon fly, wagon sheet, and everything in the wagon that got wet. Clean up Dutch ovens that got wet and rusted; grease them. You want to keep Dutch ovens dry if at all possible when not using them.

After drying everything out, we put it back in the wagon or where we have it stored in the barn. Ken, Sue, and Peggy do lots of hard work before and after going to a cooking or cook-off.

Sue, edited by Jean

BAKED BEANS

1 large can Van Camp's pork and
    beans
4 slices bacon, slightly cooked
1 small onion, sliced and ringed

½ c. brown sugar
3 Tbsp. mustard
5 Tbsp. catsup

Spray casserole dish with Pam. Fry bacon slightly. Mix pork and beans, brown sugar, mustard, and catsup; mix well. Add bacon and rings of onions. Bake at 400° for 30 minutes.

BROCCOLI AND RICE CASSEROLE

1 medium chopped onion
¼ c. oleo
1 (10 oz.) pkg. frozen chopped
    broccoli

1 can cream of mushroom soup
1 c. cooked rice
1 small jar Cheez Whiz (regular)
1 tsp. salt

Saute onion in oleo. Mix all together and put in casserole and bake at 350° about 30 minutes or until cheese browns.

CORN DISH

½ c. oleo
8 oz. pkg. cream cheese
2 cans whole kernel corn

1 (4 oz.) can chopped green chilies
Garlic salt
Salt and pepper

Melt oleo and cream cheese. Add corn, green chilies, garlic salt, salt, and pepper to taste. Bake at 350° for about 20 minutes.

CREAMY CORN

2 gal. corn
½ c. oleo
2 c. (or more) milk

8 tsp. sugar
Salt to taste
Black pepper to taste

Drain corn and add milk, oleo, sugar, salt, and black pepper in a large Dutch oven or big pan. Bring to a boil.

DUTCH OVEN FRIED POTATOES WITH ONIONS

10 potatoes
2 onions
Oil

Salt
Pepper
Garlic powder

Peel and cut up potatoes for frying (to each his own - as everyone has their own way to cut up pan-fried potatoes). Peel and slice onions. Heat small amount of oil in Dutch oven or cast iron skillet. Add potatoes. Add onion slices on top. Add salt, pepper, and garlic powder. Put on lid. Stir occasionally to keep from sticking. When done, drain off excess oil. Serve out of Dutch oven or cast iron skillet. Will keep warm longer.

FRESH BLACK-EYED PEAS

Black-eyed peas
Onion

Pace picante sauce

Shell and snap black-eyed peas; wash well. Cover with water in saucepan. Boil 15 or 20 minutes. Drain off black water; cover with fresh water. Bring to boil. Add ½ or 1 onion, according to the amount of peas. Cook until almost done and add picante sauce. Simmer until done. Serve with corn bread.

FRESH GREEN BEANS AND NEW POTATOES

2 lb. fresh green beans
5 slices bacon
Salt and pepper

6 new potatoes
2 Tbsp. minced dried onions
1 tsp. garlic powder

Boil potatoes whole until done. Cool, then remove skins. Cut into chunks. Clean, string, and snap green beans; wash very well. Cover with water and bring to boil. Let cook for about 30 minutes. Fry bacon. Let cool and break into pieces. When beans are almost done, add bacon, potatoes, dried onions, garlic, and salt and pepper to taste. Serve with corn bread.

FRIED SWEET POTATOES

Sweet potatoes
Sugar
Cinnamon

Oil
Cast iron skillet or Dutch oven

Peel sweet potatoes. Wash and cut into bite-size chunks. Heat small amount of oil in cast iron skillet or Dutch oven. Add sweet potatoes; sprinkle with sugar and cinnamon. Turn with spatula often to keep from sticking. Keep covered while cooking. When soft, pour off excess oil and serve.

1615-94

FRIED ZUCCHINI SQUASH

Medium size zucchini squash
Salt
Cooking oil

Waxed paper
Yellow corn meal

Peel as much zucchini squash as needed. Slice 1/8 to 1/4 inch slices. Spread out waxed paper and sprinkle waxed paper with salt. Lay out squash slices, 1 by 1. Sprinkle top side of squash with salt; turn each slice into corn meal and fry until golden brown on each side. Drain on paper towel.

GRANDMAW MYRTLE CATES FRIED GREEN TOMATOES

Green tomatoes
1/2 c. flour
1/2 c. corn meal

Salt
Pepper
Oil

Wash green tomatoes; slice into 1/4 inch slices. Lay out waxed paper; salt and pepper the waxed paper. Lay out tomato slices on waxed paper. Sprinkle top side of tomatoes with salt and pepper. Mix flour and corn meal together; roll tomato slices in dry mixture and fry in medium hot oil.

THE LION

Dad was an ornery cuss! Once in his younger days he was living in Turkey, Texas when a circus came to town. Now there was this "simple fellow" living there who would do anything (just about) for a jug of whisky.

With the circus was an old lion in a cage that has not been cleaned out for a very long time, and the lion's tail was hanging out of the cage. Daddy told this feller that if he could grab hold of that lion's tail and hold it - he would give him a jug of whisky!

Well, this feller grabbed the lion's tail and put his feet up on the cage and held on for dear life. The old lion roared and roared but could not get a toe hold because his cage was so dirty and he kept sliding back and forth in the muck! The circus people came running to see what the commotion was all about.

About this time, the sheriff arrived and when he saw Daddy, he knew immediately he had something to do with the situation. Daddy denied it, of course, but when they went inside the tent, this "simple fellow" saw Daddy and said, "Have I held him long enough, Dick?"

Jean, edited by Sue

1615-94

IRON SKILLET POTATOES

4 medium potatoes, sliced thin
1 medium onion, sliced

1 tsp. salt
¼ tsp. black pepper

Heat 4 tablespoons oil in iron skillet over low heat. Add potatoes, onion, salt, and black pepper. Cover and cook 20 minutes. At this time, add about ¼ cup water; replace lid and continue cooking very slowly until potatoes are tender. Stir once or twice to keep potatoes cooking without getting too brown on 1 side.

LICKIN' GOOD GREEN BEANS

2 gal. green beans
1 lb. bacon

Salt to taste
Crushed chilies (optional)

Pour all water off the green beans and wash them. Put bacon (cut into pieces) in large Dutch oven and cook a few minutes. Add green beans, water, salt, and crushed chilies. Cook very slow - just above a simmer - for about 2 hours.

MOTHER'S MACARONI AND TOMATOES

2 c. dried macaroni
1 large can tomatoes

1 can water
Salt and pepper to taste

Add macaroni to 2 quarts boiling water and 1 teaspoon salt; cook until tender. Drain and add 1 large can tomatoes (chopped) and 1 can water. Add salt and pepper to taste.

Variations: Use Velveeta cheese instead of tomatoes. Can also add picante sauce to taste.

NELDEHNS BEANS

1 lb. dried pinto beans
2 lb. lean ground beef
2 Tbsp. chili powder

Salt and pepper to taste
2 c. water

Pick through beans. Wash very well; cover with water in pot and soak overnight. Next day, bring to boil in water soaked in, then simmer until almost done.

Brown ground beef. Add water, chili powder, and salt and pepper to taste. Simmer 30 minutes, then add almost cooked beans.

Can be increased to fit size of feeding. Also, cook at chuck wagon.

ONION RINGS

Onions
1 c. buttermilk
1 c. beer
Oil
1 c. flour

1 c. corn meal
1 tsp. salt
1/4 tsp. black pepper
1/4 tsp. red (cayenne) pepper

Peel and slice onions into 1/4 or 3/8 inch slices; separate into rings. Dip rings into mixture of buttermilk and beer. Roll in flour, corn meal, salt, and peppers. Fry in deep hot fat. Drain well and serve warm.

PINTO BEANS

2 c. pinto beans
1 1/2 c. cold water
1/2 lb. salt pork or bacon, cut up
1 red chili pepper
1 1/2 Tbsp. chili powder
1 clove garlic, minced

1 medium onion, chopped
3 oz. tomato paste
1 tsp. salt
1 tsp. ground cumin
1/2 tsp. marjoram

Soak beans overnight. Put into bean pot next morning and bring to a boil; reduce heat. Cover and simmer 1 hour. Add other ingredients; cover and simmer 3 more hours or until done. Add water as necessary.

QUICK SPANISH RICE

4 slices bacon
1 green pepper
1 clove garlic
1 medium onion
5 oz. pkg. precooked rice

1 (10 1/2 oz.) can tomato soup
1 can water
1/2 tsp. salt
1 tsp. chili powder (or to taste)

Chop bacon, green pepper, and garlic; cut onion in slices. Fry bacon in large skillet until almost crisp. Add onion, green pepper, garlic, and rice. Cook over medium heat until vegetables are slightly browned. Add tomato soup, water, salt, and chili powder. Turn heat to low and simmer 10 to 12 minutes. Serve with enchilada casserole or enchiladas.

SPINACH CASSEROLE

2 pkg. chopped spinach
2 (3 oz.) ctn. cream cheese
1 can mushroom soup

35 Ritz crackers
1 can onion rings (Durkee)
1/2 c. margarine

Cook spinach as directed on package; drain well. Soften cream cheese and then mix well with the mushroom soup. Add this to the spinach. Put in a buttered casserole dish; top with 1/2 can onion rings. Crush Ritz crackers and add margarine. Place on top of spinach/onion layer. Put remainder of onion rings on top, mashing down slightly. Bake at 350° for 30 minutes.

SQUASH CASSEROLE

1 or 2 yellow squash
1 large onion, sliced
4 oz. can chopped green chilies
Oleo

Salt and pepper
4 or 5 slices cheese
8 or 10 Ritz crackers

Slice 1 layer of squash in a casserole dish. Layer sliced onion, then sprinkle green chilies on that. Add another layer of squash, onion, and green chilies. Salt and pepper; dot with oleo. Cover with cheese, then crush Ritz crackers on top. Bake at 350° about 1 hour or until squash and onion is tender.

SWEET POTATO CASSEROLE

3 eggs, beaten
3 c. mashed sweet potatoes
½ c. sugar

⅓ c. milk
1 Tbsp. vanilla extract
½ c. melted margarine

Topping:

1 c. brown sugar
⅔ c. flour

1 c. chopped pecans
½ c. margarine

Lightly beat the eggs. Mix sweet potatoes, sugar, milk, vanilla, beaten eggs, and margarine together. Spoon into a buttered 13x9 inch casserole dish. Combine brown sugar, flour, pecans, and margarine by blending with a pastry blender or your fingers. Sprinkle over the sweet potato mixture. Bake at 350° for 30 minutes.

Main

Dishes

Justin Wells
94

MEAT ROASTING GUIDE

Cut	Weight Pounds	Approx. Time (Hours) (325° oven)	Internal Temperature
BEEF			
Standing rib roast			
(10 inch) ribs	4	1¾	140° (rare)
(If using shorter cut (8-inch)		2	160° (medium)
ribs, allow 30 min. longer)		2½	170° (well done)
	8	2½	140° (rare)
		3	160° (medium)
		4½	170° (well done)
Rolled ribs	4	2	140° (rare)
		2½	160° (medium)
		3	170° (well done)
	6	3	140° (rare)
		3¼	160° (medium)
		4	170° (well done)
Rolled rump	5	2¼	140° (rare)
(Roast only if high quality.	3	160° (medium)	
Otherwise, braise.)		3¼	170° (well done)
Sirloin tip	3	1½	140° (rare)
(Roast only if high quality.		2	160° (medium)
Otherwise, braise.)		2¼	170° (well done)
LAMB			
Leg	6	3	175° (medium)
		3½	180° (well done)
	8	4	175° (medium)
		4½	180° (well done)
VEAL			
Leg (piece)	5	2½ to 3	170° (well done)
Shoulder	6	3½	170° (well done)
Rolled shoulder	3 to 5	3 to 3½	170° (well done)

POULTRY ROASTING GUIDE

Type of Poultry	Ready-To-Cook Weight	Oven Temperature	Approx. Total Roasting Time
TURKEY	6 to 8 lb.	325°	2½ to 3 hr.
	8 to 12 lb.	325°	3 to 3½ hr.
	12 to 16 lb.	325°	3½ to 4 hr.
	16 to 20 lb.	325°	4 to 4½ hr.
	20 to 24 lb.	300°	5 to 6 hr.
CHICKEN	2 to 2½ lb.	400°	1 to 1½ hr.
(Unstuffed)	2½ to 4 lb.	400°	1½ to 2½ hr.
	4 to 8 lb.	325°	3 to 5 hr.
DUCK	3 to 5 lb.	325°	2½ to 3 hr.
(Unstuffed)			

NOTE: Small chickens are roasted at 400° so that they brown well in the short cooking time. They may also be done at 325° but will take longer and will not be as brown. Increase cooking time 15 to 20 minutes for stuffed chicken and duck.

MAIN DISHES

POTS, PANS, AND EQUIPMENT

In chuckwagon cook-offs, we use cast iron Dutch ovens. When roasting meat and baking bread or cobblers, you need Dutch ovens that have 3 legs and a flange lid that holds coals to make an oven. Dig a shallow hole slightly larger than the Dutch oven; place hot coals in the hole. Place the oven on the coals in the hole; cover the lid and pile more hot coals over all.

If the wind is blowing, tone down the coals by adding ashes. Flat bottom Dutch ovens are used in your camp ovens or in your kitchen oven at home. We have size 5 inch to 16 inch Dutch ovens but several of the larger ones. You need a lot when you are required to cook for 40 to 80 people in a cook-off.

Some chuckwagons have metal wood burning camp stoves that have burners on top and a regular oven. They carry them especially if they are going to be set up for a week or more.

Old stuff needed for a cook-off:

Old pots
Dish pans
Bread pan
Tin plates
Granite coffee pots
Granite or tin cups
Forks, knives, and spoons of
    German silver, steel, or steel
    with wood or bone handles
Water bucket
Long handled dipper
Wash pan
Metal cans with tight fitting lids
Sourdough crocks
Flour sacks (for dish towels)
Meat saw
Cleaver

Clock
Pot hooks
Pot racks (to set over fire)
Heavy hammer
Single bit axe
Two-man crosscut saw
Brace and bit
Water barrel
Kerosene lanterns
Stake pins
Rawhide and rope hobbles
Rope horse pins
Cowboy tepees
Bedrolls
Harness (to put on the wagon
    tongue)

If we are cooking for a catered meal for 100 people or more, we use a big wash pot to cook meat in that will hold 1 hundred pounds of meat. We have 2 of them. We use 21 quart and 33 quart pans to cook other foods in. The most we have cooked for on this chuckwagon is 400 people.

Sue, edited by Jean

AUNT EULA MAE HODGES TATER TOT CASSEROLE

1½ lb. ground meat
1 onion, chopped
1 bell pepper, chopped
1 can cream of mushroom or cream
    of chicken soup

1 soup can milk
1 (2 lb.) pkg. tater tots, thawed

Brown meat; drain. Saute onions and bell pepper in oleo and add to ground meat. Add soup and milk; cook together a few minutes. Line casserole dish with thawed tater tots. Pour meat mixture over tater tots. Put more tater tots on top and bake at 350° until tater tots are brown and mixture bubbles. *Very good.*

AUNT OLA LISENBY'S RAVIOLI

6 large chicken breasts
1 large or 2 small onions, chopped
    fine
1 large bell pepper, chopped fine

1 jar chopped pimientos
2 cans cream of mushroom soup
    (undiluted)
12 oz. egg noodles

Boil and bone chicken. Saute onions and bell pepper in oleo until tender. Boil noodles in chicken broth. Add enough water to keep from sticking. Add 1 tablespoon oleo and cook until tender. Add onions, bell pepper, pimientos, chicken, and mushroom soup; stir very carefully where it won't tear.

Put in a buttered casserole and bake at 350° for 15 to 20 minutes. When it's bubbly, cover with mild grated cheese and cook just long enough to melt.

Note: An original recipe of Liberace.

BAKED STEAK AND VEGETABLES

1 round steak
6 potatoes, peeled and sliced
6 carrots, peeled and sliced
1 onion, sliced

½ bell pepper, sliced
Salt and pepper to taste
Garlic salt to taste
Tenderizer

Cut round steak into pieces; season with tenderizer, salt, pepper, and garlic salt. Layer steak, potatoes, onion, carrots, and bell pepper in a 9x13 inch baking pan. Salt and pepper. Seal with foil and bake 1 hour at 350°.

BBQ SPARERIBS
(Cook out or in)

Spareribs   Favorite BBQ sauce

Cut spareribs into 1 or 2 ribs and cook in pressure cooker (rocking) for 10 minutes. Run cold water over lid to cool cooker before removing lid. Remove spareribs. Put outdoors on grill and baste with your favorite BBQ sauce over low heat coals.

Can also be cooked slowly in your oven instead of on grill.

BEEF AND BEAN BURRITO

1 lb. ground chuck
1 small onion, chopped
1 (4 oz.) can green chilies
Salt and pepper to taste

1 Tbsp. Worcestershire sauce
1 can Ranch Style beans
Flour tortillas

Brown ground chuck and onion. Add green chilies, salt, pepper, Worcestershire sauce, and beans. Let ingredients warm and roll in flour tortilla.

BEEF AND POTATO LOAF

1. Arrange evenly in a greased iron skillet 4 cups thinly sliced, peeled raw potatoes and 1 tablespoon chopped onion. Sprinkle with 1 teaspoon salt, 1/8 teaspoon pepper, and 1 teaspoon parsley flakes.
2. Mix 1 pound ground beef, 3/4 cup can milk, 1/2 cup cracker crumbs or uncooked oats, 1/4 cup catsup or chili sauce, 1/4 cup chopped onion, 1 teaspoon salt, and 1/8 teaspoon pepper. Spread evenly over potatoes.
3. Decorate top with more catsup if desired. Bake in 350° oven 1 hour or until potatoes are tender.

BEEF FAJITAS

¾ c. lime juice
½ c. cooking oil
1 (4 oz.) can chopped green chilies
½ c. Worcestershire sauce
Dash of hot sauce

½ tsp. salt
1 onion, thinly sliced
1 (1½ to 2½ lb.) beef skirt or flank
   steak
8 inch flour tortillas

Mix together lime juice, oil, green chilies, Worcestershire sauce, hot sauce, salt, and onion. Place steak in a shallow dish. Pour marinade over it and cover. Refrigerate overnight or 8 to 10 hours. Turn it several times.

When ready to grill, remove from marinade; reserve marinade. Pat steak dry with paper towels. With a slotted spoon, remove the onion and green chilies from marinade and wrap them in foil. Put the chilies and onion on to cook the same time you do the steak. Grill the steak over medium heat for 9 to 10 minutes. Turn steak and continue grilling until done to taste. Brush steak occasionally with reserved marinade during grilling. To serve, bias slice steak into thin strips. Put on warmed tortilla.

BEEF STEW

2 lb. stew meat, cut up
1 chopped onion
1 tsp. salt
¼ tsp. black pepper
1 Tbsp. chili powder
½ tsp. garlic salt

Water (to cover)
6 potatoes, peeled and diced
2 (16 oz.) cans tomatoes
2 (8 oz.) cans tomato sauce
1 can Veg-All or mixed vegetables

Cook stew meat, onion, salt, black pepper, chili powder, and garlic salt in a small Dutch oven or bean pot. Cook about 1 hour or until meat is tender. Cook potatoes until tender; drain. Add potatoes, tomatoes, tomato sauce, and mixed vegetables to meat mixture; bring to a boil.

BRISKET

3 to 6 lb. brisket
Onion salt
Garlic salt

Seasoning salt
½ bottle liquid smoke
½ c. lemon juice

Bar-B-Que Sauce:

1 c. ketchup
½ c. Worcestershire sauce

2 Tbsp. brown sugar
Tabasco

Sprinkle onion, garlic, and seasoning salts on both sides of brisket and pour ½ bottle liquid smoke over brisket; wrap tightly in heavy foil and place in 300° oven. Allow 1 hour per pound.

Take out of oven. Drain off all juice. Pour ½ cup lemon juice and some Bar-B-Que Sauce over meat. Put back in oven and cook, uncovered, 30 to 45 minutes. Slices better when cold.

BRISKET

8 to 10 lb. brisket
6 to 8 slices bacon
Unseasoned meat tenderizer

Garlic powder
Black pepper

Trim excess fat from brisket; sprinkle all sides with tenderizer, garlic powder, and black pepper. Put on rack of deep broiling pan to catch excess liquid. Add strips of bacon and cover tightly with heavy foil. Cook 4 to 5 hours until done at 225°. Can be served chopped as a brisket salad.

BUNK HOUSE MEAT LOAF

3 lb. ground beef
1 lb. ground pork
½ c. finely chopped onion
½ c. chopped green pepper
3 eggs

1 c. cooked oatmeal
1½ c. cracker crumbs
½ c. ketchup
3 Tbsp. salt
½ tsp. pepper

Mix ingredients. Place in greased loaf pans. Bake at 350° for 1½ hours.

CABBAGE PATCH STEW

1 lb. lean ground beef
1 large onion, chopped
1 green pepper, chopped
2 large ribs celery, chopped
1 (16 oz.) can tomatoes
1 (16 oz.) can Ranch Style beans

1 medium head cabbage, cut up
½ c. water
1 Tbsp. chili powder
½ jalapeno pepper (optional)
Salt and pepper to taste

Crumble ground beef into a Dutch oven; cook until browned. Add onion, pepper, and celery; cook until softened. Stir in remaining ingredients. Cover and cook on medium-low for approximately 30 minutes.

Note: This is an unusual sounding recipe but the flavor combination is very good and it makes a large recipe. Extra water can be added if a juicier product is desired.

CALF FRIES

Calf fries
1 c. buttermilk
1 c. beer
Cooking oil

2 c. flour
2 c. corn meal
Salt
Pepper

Peel calf fries. They peel better if they are slightly frozen. Cut into bite-size pieces. Rinse with cold water. Dip into mixture of buttermilk and beer, then roll in mixture of flour, corn meal, salt, and pepper. Fry in deep hot oil. Drain grease and serve.

1615-94

CALF FRIES

Calf fries
1 c. flour
1 c. corn meal

Salt
Pepper
Oil

Peel calf fries. Rinse with cold water. Roll into mixture of corn meal, flour, salt, and pepper. Fry in hot fat. Drain and serve.

CHICKEN AND BROCCOLI CASSEROLE

6 chicken breasts
3 large pkg. frozen broccoli or 3 to
   4 lb. fresh broccoli
2 cans cream of chicken soup (do
   not dilute)

½ c. sour cream
½ c. mayonnaise
½ c. grated Cheddar cheese
1 small can Durkee dried onions
2 c. grated Cheddar cheese

Cook chicken breasts; debone and cut into bite-size pieces. Cut broccoli into bite-size pieces and cook. Grease a 13x9 inch baking dish. Place broccoli on the bottom and cover with the chicken pieces. Mix together the soup, sour cream, mayonnaise, and ½ cup cheese. Spread this mixture evenly over the chicken and broccoli. Sprinkle dried onions and 2 cups grated cheese over that. Bake in a 350° oven for 20 to 30 minutes or until hot and cheese is completely melted.

CHICKEN ENCHILADAS

1 large chicken
1 c. chopped onion
1 clove garlic
2 Tbsp. butter
1 (16 oz.) can tomatoes
1 (8 oz.) can tomato sauce
1 (4 oz.) can green chilies

1 Tbsp. sugar
½ tsp. salt
½ tsp. oregano
½ tsp. basil
1 (8 oz.) ctn. sour cream
Corn tortillas
Grated cheese

Cook and debone chicken. Combine in a saucepan the onion, garlic, butter, tomatoes, tomato sauce, green chilies, sugar, salt, oregano, and basil; cook for 15 minutes or longer. Add sour cream.

Fill corn tortillas with chicken and grated cheese; put in a 9x13 inch baking dish. Cover with sauce mixture and bake for 30 minutes. Sprinkle with cheese and bake another 10 minutes.

CHICKEN FLAUTAS

2 c. chopped cooked chicken
⅔ c. hot sauce
¼ c. green onion slices
¾ tsp. ground cumin

Vegetable oil
32 corn tortillas
2 c. shredded cheese
Guacamole

Combine chicken, hot sauce, onion, and cumin; mix well. Heat about ½ inch oil in small skillet until hot but not smoking. Quickly fry each tortilla in oil to soften, about 2 seconds on each side. Drain on paper towels. Spoon 1 tablespoon chicken mixture and 1 tablespoon cheese down center of each tortilla. Roll tightly; secure with a wooden pick.

Place seam-side down on baking sheet. Bake in preheated oven at 400° about 18 to 20 minutes or until crisp. Serve warm with guacamole and additional hot sauce. Makes 32 appetizers.

CHICKEN FRIED STEAK

1 to 2 lb. round steak, tenderized
Sprinkle of garlic salt
Sprinkle of tenderizer
Some black pepper

1 egg
½ c. milk
1 c. flour

Cut steak into serving size pieces. Season steak with tenderizer, garlic salt, and black pepper. Beat egg and milk together. Put a little soda in the egg mixture for a golden color. Roll steaks in flour, then egg-milk mixture. Roll in flour again and fry in hot lard.

CHICKEN SPAGHETTI

1 hen
1 large can tomatoes
1 jar mushrooms, chopped
1 box uncut spaghetti

1 onion, chopped
1 tsp. chili powder
1 lb. grated cheese (red rind is the best)

Boil hen; cool. Remove flesh from bone and cut into small pieces. Cook spaghetti in broth of chicken for 15 minutes. Cook chopped onion in tomatoes until tender. Add chili powder. Add mushrooms to spaghetti. Mix all ingredients and add salt and pepper to suit taste. (Do not have too soupy.) Serve hot and top each serving with grated cheese.

1615-94

CHUCKWAGON BEEF STEW

4 lb. lean beef, cubed
4 Tbsp. oil
2 cloves garlic
4 c. hot water
2 large cans tomatoes
2 thin slices lemon
4 medium onions, sliced
2 Tbsp. salt

½ tsp. pepper
6 Tbsp. sugar
12 medium carrots, peeled and cut
    into 1 inch pieces
9 to 10 medium potatoes, quartered
Dash of cloves
½ tsp. dried basil leaves
2 cans English peas

Brown beef well in hot oil in Dutch oven or skillet. Remove and put into pot. Add garlic, mixing well. Add water, tomatoes, lemon, onions, salt, pepper, and sugar. Mix well and simmer 2 hours, stirring occasionally. Add carrots, potatoes, cloves, and crushed basil leaves. Cover and cook until vegetables are tender. Add canned peas and heat. If necessary, to thicken gravy, thicken with flour, dissolved in water. Serve hot.

COWBOY HOTDISH

1 lb. hamburger
½ c. chopped onion
½ c. chopped green pepper
2 (16 oz.) cans pork and beans
½ c. molasses

½ c. ketchup
½ tsp. dry mustard
1 tsp. salt
1 Tbsp. Worcestershire sauce

Brown hamburger, onion, and green pepper. Add pork and beans, molasses, ketchup, dry mustard, salt, and Worcestershire sauce; mix well. Put into 2 quart baking dish and bake at 375° for 30 minutes or you may also use a crock pot.

CURTIS' T-BONE STEAK GRILLED

T-bone steaks
Liquid smoke

Salt
Pepper

Brush steak lightly with liquid smoke. Grease grill (very lightly), just enough to keep from sticking. Salt and pepper grill. Brown steak on both sides on medium hot grill. Serve hot.

Curtis won an award with this steak in 4-H.

DADDY'S BEEF FOR 50 PEOPLE

35 lb. boneless chuck
4 oz. tenderizer
4 (18 oz.) bottles Kraft Bar-B-Que
    sauce

Water

Cut boneless chuck roast into 1½ inch cubes. Put meat into a wash pot and set it on a hot fire. Add tenderizer and Bar-B-Que sauce. Add enough water and liquid to cover the meat. Stir to distribute ingredients. After it comes to a boil, cook slow until it is extremely tender, 3 or 4 hours. The slower the cooking, the better the flavor.

DADDY'S SON-OF-A-GUN STEW

½ the heart
½ the spleen
¼ the liver
All the tongue

All the sweetbreads
Marrow gut (about 3 feet)
All the butchers steak
1 set brains

From a freshly killed beef, take the following: Heart, spleen, liver, tongue, sweetbreads, marrow gut, butchers steak, and brains. Wash them very well. Cut into pieces suitable for stew. Put them into a Dutch oven with a small (1 inch square) of suet tallow. Cover with water. Season with salt, pepper, and chili powder. Boil until meat is tender. Add a handful of flour (adding warm water if necessary). Stir until mixture cooks for ½ hour. Serve.

DUCKLING

Duckling
1 apple

Salt and pepper
Paprika

Rinse under water. Rub inside and out with salt, pepper, and paprika. Put apple inside duckling. Score the skin with knife at 1 inch intervals. Roast duck whole, *uncovered,* until skin is crisp and brown. Serve with Brown and Wild Rice Stuffing and Apricot-Almond Sauce.

DUCKLING BROWN AND WILD RICE STUFFING

1 c. celery
¼ c. duck fat
4 oz. uncooked wild rice
¼ tsp. salt
⅓ c. chopped green onions

⅔ c. uncooked brown rice
3 Tbsp. parsley flakes
⅛ tsp. paprika
2 c. water

Mix together and simmer until rice is cooked. Serve with duck and Apricot-Almond Sauce.

1615-94

DUCKLING APRICOT-ALMOND SAUCE

2 Tbsp. cornstarch
1 (No. 303) can apricot halves,
   drained
½ c. slivered almonds
1 Tbsp. vinegar

½ c. sugar
1 tsp. soy sauce
1⅓ c. giblet broth
Cooked giblets and neck meat (no
   liver)

Combine cornstarch, sugar, vinegar, and soy sauce. Add to juices and cook over low heat until mixture thickens. Add cooked, chopped giblets and neck meats. Add almond and apricots. Serve sauce over duckling with Wild and Brown Rice Stuffing.

DUTCH OVEN BEEF LOAF

¾ c. milk
1 egg
1½ c. bread crumbs
1 tsp. salt
½ tsp. oregano

1 small chopped onion
1 c. catsup
2 lb. lean ground beef
1 Tbsp. brown sugar
1 Tbsp. Worcestershire sauce

Combine milk, egg, bread crumbs, salt, oregano, and onion with ground beef; mix well. Pat into well-greased 12 inch Dutch oven. Bake on medium coals 1 hour. Combine catsup, brown sugar, and Worcestershire sauce; bring to a boil. Pour on beef loaf and bake 10 more minutes.

DUTCH OVEN POT ROAST

12 lb. chuck roast
8 tsp. salt
Tenderizer
Johnny B's seasoning

16 potatoes, peeled and quartered
4 onions, peeled and quartered
2 pkg. carrots, peeled
8 Tbsp. shortening

Melt shortening in 16 inch Dutch oven. Rub seasoning, tenderizer, and salt on roast; brown in Dutch oven, turning once. Reduce heat by moving the oven from fire to bed of coals. Let cook very slow, about 1½ to 2 hours. Add carrots and onions; continue cooking until meat is tender. Add potatoes about the last hour. A small amount of water may be added, if necessary, while cooking.

DUTCH OVEN SMOTHERED STEAK

Round steak
Flour
Beer or water or mixture

Onions, sliced
Grease

Beat steak to tenderize; salt and roll in flour. Brown on both sides in Dutch oven with small amount of grease until all steak is browned. Put steak back in Dutch oven. Add liquid of your choice to top of steak. Add sliced onions (optional). Cover with lid and cook until steak is tender and onions are done.

EASY TAMALE PIE

1 chopped onion
1 lb. ground beef
2 c. canned tomatoes
2 c. cream style corn
1 c. milk
2 c. uncooked yellow corn meal

1½ tsp. salt
1½ tsp. chili powder
1½ c. black olives
½ lb. shredded Monterey Jack cheese

In a large heavy skillet, brown ground beef and onion. Stir in tomatoes, corn, milk, corn meal, salt, and chili powder. Top with olives and cheese. Cover and cook on top of stove on low heat, about 20 to 25 minutes. Serves 6 to 8.

ENCHILADAS

2 lb. ground beef
1 Tbsp. chili powder
1 tsp. salt
½ tsp. black pepper
1 tsp. cumin
1 tsp. coriander
1 small onion

1 garlic bud
24 corn tortillas
2 cans chicken broth
1 c. water
1 Tbsp. chili powder
Salt to taste
3 Tbsp. flour

Brown ground beef. Add chopped onion, garlic, and spices; simmer about 10 minutes. Dip corn tortillas into hot grease quickly. Roll meat mixture into tortillas and arrange in cake pan. Brown flour in small amount of grease. Add water and stir, then add broth and spices. Simmer about 10 minutes. Pour mixture over enchiladas. Bake at 350° until bubbly. Top with grated cheese. Serve with Spanish rice and pinto beans.

ENCHILADA CASSEROLE

2 lb. lean ground beef
1 onion, chopped
2 Tbsp. chili powder
2 tsp. garlic powder
1 c. diced green chilies
1 can enchilada sauce

1 can cream of mushroom soup
1 can evaporated milk
1 pkg. tortilla chips
2 c. grated cheese
½ c. grated cheese (for topping)
Chopped green onion

Brown ground beef. Add chopped onion, chili powder, and garlic powder. In large bowl, mix green chilies, enchilada sauce, soup, and milk. Line bottom of 9x13 inch cake pan with tortilla chips. Add layer of meat and layer of cheese. Repeat layers until all is used, making layer of chips last. Pour liquid mixture over top. Bake 30 to 40 minutes at 350° (until bubbly). Sprinkle cheese and chopped green onion over top.

1615-94

FORGOTTEN SHORT RIBS

3 lb. beef short ribs
1½ tsp. salt
½ tsp. pepper
1 (8 oz.) can tomato sauce

2 Tbsp. light molasses
2 Tbsp. cider vinegar
1 tsp. liquid smoke
1 Tbsp. instant minced onion

Sprinkle ribs with salt and pepper. Place in a Dutch oven or a 3 quart casserole. In a small pan, combine tomato sauce, molasses, vinegar, liquid smoke, and minced onion. Bring to a boil and then simmer for 5 minutes; pour over ribs. Cover and bake in a 275° oven for 3 to 4 hours or until tender.

FRIED CHICKEN AND CREAM GRAVY

1 frying chicken
½ c. milk
¼ tsp. soda
1 egg
Flour
Salt

4 Tbsp. grease (from frying chicken)
4 Tbsp. flour
1 can canned milk
1 can water
Salt and pepper to taste

Mix milk, soda, and egg together. Salt cut up fryer; roll in flour. Dip in egg mixture and again in flour. Fry in medium heat until golden brown. Turn to other side. Remove from grease and drain on rack or paper towels.

Use grease left from chicken. Brown flour mixture. Add canned milk and water; cook until desired thickness, stirring constantly. Add salt and pepper to taste.

GOLDEN PORK CHOPS

8 pork chops
¾ c. fine bread crumbs

1 pkg. golden onion soup mix

Preheat oven to 375°. Rinse pork chops. Mix soup mix and bread crumbs. Place pork chops in this mixture coating on both sides and place on a greased cookie sheet. Cook 20 minutes; turn and cook 15 minutes more. Serve with chilled applesauce! *Yum. Yum.*

GOOD STUFF MEAT DISH

1 pkg. Williams chili blend
2 lb. ground beef
1 large can tomatoes
½ onion, chopped

1 tsp. minced garlic
1 pkg. noodles or shellroni
1 c. grated cheese
Salt and pepper to taste

Brown ground beef; drain off excess fat. Add chili blend, onion, and garlic. Chop tomatoes and add juice and all; simmer 30 minutes. Cook noodles as directed; drain and rinse. Add to meat stuff. Mix and add grated cheese to top and put lid on pot. Cheese will melt. Serve hot. Add extra spices if desired.

LITTLE ROWDY

All five of us grew up riding a little paint horse named "Little Rowdy." Mother, Daddy, and our Garner grandparents were raising paint horses at the time. "Little Rowdy" came from big parents but his growth was stunted and he was only about 14 hands.

He was about 14 or 15 years old - the same age as our brother Frank - by the time Sue and I were big enough to saddle him. Even then it took both of us. We would ride him to church and when we would come out after evening services, our saddle would be turned around backwards. We always knew Bob Hunnicutt and Pete Smith had something to do with that but they would never own up to it!

He was our trick horse! We could get him to rear up like "Trigger" - Roy Roger's horse. Sue and Frank could stand on him and spin a rope.

We would ride him double to town and turn him loose on a vacant space between 2 buildings. He would stay there and wait for us unless it was one of the days the ice cream truck came to town with dry ice on it. On those days, someone would always put dry ice in a fruit jar, screw the lid on tight, and the jar would explode! "Little Rowdy" would then head for home!

One time someone stole him and he was gone for 2 weeks before Pat Edwards found him tied to a fence about 15 miles from home. I knew then God did answer prayer because I had prayed daily for him. "Little Rowdy" lived to be 28 years old.

Jean, edited by Sue

GREEN CHILI CASSEROLE

2 lb. ground beef
½ onion, chopped
2 cans cream of chicken soup
1 large sour cream

1 or 1½ soup cans water
2 cans diced green chilies
1 pkg. tortilla chips
1 c. grated cheese

Spray 13x9 inch oblong cake pan with Pam for easier cleaning. Brown beef and drain off excess fat. Add onion. Let simmer a few minutes. In saucepan, mix soup, sour cream, green chilies, and water. Heat while stirring constantly. Crumble some tortilla chips to cover bottom of pan. Add meat mixture. Add more chips on top. Pour liquid over top. Let go down into casserole. Heat 25 to 30 minutes until bubbly. Remove from oven and add grated cheese.

GREEN CHILI STEW

2 lb. lean pork
6 whole green chilies
5 medium potatoes
2 Tbsp. chicken bouillon granules
1 tsp. cumin

1 tsp. coriander
1 tsp. onion powder
1 tsp. garlic powder
1 tsp. chili powder

Use fresh or canned green chilies. If fresh, fry in grease until skin turns white. Remove and let set until cool and then peel. Cut up pork into bite-size pieces and brown in small amount of grease.

In large pot, cover pork with water. Bring to boil, then simmer 30 minutes. Add sliced potatoes, bouillon, spices, and cut up green chilies; simmer until potatoes are done. May add additional spices to taste.

HOMEMADE CHILI

2 lb. ground beef
1 chopped onion
2 tsp. salt
Dash of garlic salt
1 tsp. chili powder

4 Tbsp. chili caribe (ground chilies)
1 (16 oz.) can tomatoes
1 (8 oz.) can tomato sauce
1 (15 oz.) can Ranch Style beans
1 c. water

In Dutch oven, brown beef and onion; drain. Add all other ingredients and bring to a boil. Cover and simmer 25 to 30 minutes. Add water if needed.

HOMEMADE CHOW MEIN

2 lb. leftover roast beef (more or
    less)
1 onion, chopped large
3 stalks celery, sliced

Corn starch (to thicken)
1 can bean sprouts
1 can water chestnuts
1 can mixed Chinese vegetables

Slice roast beef thinly and into bite-size pieces. Boil with onion and celery for 5 minutes. Drain and rinse very well the bean sprouts, water chestnuts, and mixed vegetables. Add to beef mixture; bring to boil and thicken with corn starch, dissolved in cold water. Add to boiling mixture until desired thickness. Serve over rice. Top with chow mein noodles and soy sauce to taste.

INDIAN STEW

2 Tbsp. fat
1 onion, chopped
½ green pepper, chopped
1 lb. lean hamburger
Pinch of chili powder

3 c. fresh corn
1 can tomato soup
1 tsp. sugar
1 tsp. salt

Heat fat in iron skillet and cook onion and green pepper until soft. Brown meat. Add remaining ingredients and simmer for 1 hour. Serves 4 to 6.

LEAN BEEF SAUSAGE

1 lb. lean ground beef
½ to 1 tsp. salt
½ tsp. crushed red pepper pods
¼ tsp. ground black pepper
¼ tsp. ground white pepper

1 tsp. fennel seeds (optional)
2 tsp. rubbed, dried sage
Additional mixed spices (thyme,
    marjoram, rosemary, basil) to
    total 3 tsp.

Here is a real treat for those who like a breakfast sausage, but must avoid fatty meats. They're so lean that you might need to spray or grease the skillet to keep from sticking.

In a medium bowl, combine beef and spices; mix well. Shape into a log. Wrap in waxed paper. Chill for several hours or overnight. Cut into slices and slowly cook in a heavy skillet or on a griddle. Turn to brown. Can be sliced and frozen on a cookie sheet, then put in a freezer bag and used when needed.

1615-94

MEAL IN A DISH

1 lb. ground beef
1 medium onion, chopped
½ green pepper, chopped

1 (4 oz.) can green chilies, chopped
1 can Ranch Style beans
1 recipe of corn bread

Crumble beef in large skillet. Add chopped onion and pepper; let brown. Drain. Add green chilies and beans; simmer 15 minutes. Pour into large baking dish and pour recipe of corn bread over top. Bake in 350° oven for 30 to 45 minutes or until corn bread is browned.

Add a tossed salad and dessert and a meal is complete.

MEAT LOAF

2 lb. ground beef
1 chopped onion
2 eggs
½ c. chopped bell pepper
1 tsp. salt
½ tsp. black pepper
Dash of garlic salt

1 (8 oz.) can tomato sauce
¼ c. milk
3 Tbsp. picante sauce
20 crackers, crumbled
4 slices bread, pinched into small
    pieces

Mix all together and put into a sprayed 8 or 10 inch Dutch oven. Spread catsup on top. Cook on slow coals about 1 hour or until done. Can be cooked in regular oven at 350°.

MEAT LOAF

2 lb. ground beef
2 eggs
¼ c. milk
1 pkg. onion soup mix

16 corn tortilla chips
1 large can cream of mushroom
    soup

Mix ground beef, soup mix, eggs, milk, and tortilla chips. Make into loaf. Put inside foil, inside small roast pan. Pour cream of mushroom soup over top and close foil. Put lid on roaster. Bake 1 hour or until done at 350°.

MEAT AND MACARONI DISH

1 to 2 lb. hamburger meat
12 oz. pkg. elbow macaroni
1 (16 oz.) can tomatoes, chopped
2 (8 oz.) cans tomato sauce
½ c. chopped onion

1 (4 oz.) can green chilies
¼ tsp. salt
¼ tsp. black pepper
½ tsp. chili powder
¼ tsp. garlic salt

Brown hamburger meat and onion in a large iron skillet; drain. Cook macaroni as directed on package. To hamburger meat, add salt, pepper, chili powder, and garlic salt. Add green chilies, tomato sauce, and tomatoes. Simmer while macaroni is cooking. Drain macaroni and add to meat mixture.

MEXICAN CASSEROLE

1½ to 2 lb. hamburger
1 small chopped onion
Salt and pepper to taste
Chili powder to taste
1 can cream of chicken soup
1 can cream of mushroom soup

1 can evaporated milk
1 small can taco sauce
1 small can chopped green chilies
1 pkg. plain Doritos
2 c. grated cheese

Brown hamburger and onion. Season to taste with salt, pepper, and chili powder. To this, add soups, milk, taco sauce, green chilies, and Doritos. Mix all together. Pour into 9x13 inch casserole dish. Cover with cheese and bake at 350° for 20 to 30 minutes.

MEXICAN CHICKEN

1 (3 lb.) chicken, boiled, boned,
   and diced
1 can Ro-Tel tomatoes (hot)
1 can chicken broth
1 can cream of mushroom soup
1 tsp. cumin

1 tsp. oregano
½ to 1 lb. sharp cheese
2 pkg. corn tortillas
1 medium onion, finely chopped
1 can cream of chicken soup
1 Tbsp. chili powder

Saute onion in butter. Add soups, spices, and tomatoes; mix. Simmer until hot. Spray large baking dish. Line bottom with tortillas, which are quartered. Put chicken on top; cover with sauce. Sprinkle with cheese. Repeat layering until complete. Place in 350° oven to melt cheese and warm. Serves 8.

MEXICAN DISH

2 lb. hamburger meat
1 (4 oz.) can green chilies
½ chopped onion
1 (15 oz.) can Ranch Style beans

1 (15 oz.) can Ranch Style Spanish
   rice
2 c. grated cheese

Brown hamburger meat; drain. Add onion and green chilies, then beans and rice. Simmer about 15 minutes. Put cheese on top and bake in oven at 350° for about 20 minutes.

MEXICAN STYLE MACARONI

2 c. elbow macaroni
1 medium onion, finely chopped
1 can Ro-Tel tomatoes (hot)
Garlic salt to taste

1 c. grated cheese
2 Tbsp. bacon drippings
Salt and black pepper

Boil macaroni according to package directions; drain. Saute onion in drippings. Add tomatoes; stew for a few minutes. Season. Add macaroni. Remove from fire and add cheese. Serve.

MOTHER'S CANNED FRIED STEAK

Round steak
Flour

Pepper
Lard or shortening

Cut steak into frying size pieces. Sprinkle with pepper. Roll in flour; fry in hot fat. Brown on both sides. Put into fruit jars. Cover with lard. Pressure in pressure cooker to seal.

MILK GRAVY

3 Tbsp. drippings
3 Tbsp. flour

1½ c. milk (approx.)
Salt and pepper to taste

Drippings from steak, ham, pork chops, bacon, sausage, and hamburger all make the foundation for a good gravy. Can also use canned milk.

Put drippings in a saucepan over medium heat. Stirring constantly, add flour to fat or oil and brown slightly. Continue stirring to prevent scorching while slowly adding enough milk to thin mixture to a desired consistency. Season to taste.

OVEN FRIED CHICKEN

1 cut up fryer
¼ c. oleo
½ c. Bisquick

1 tsp. salt
¼ tsp. pepper
1 tsp. paprika

Mix Bisquick, salt, pepper, and paprika. Roll chicken parts in the mixture. Put in cake pan in which ¼ cup oleo has been melted. Bake in 425° oven for 35 minutes. Turn and bake for 25 minutes more. Double recipe for large chicken.

PIT BAR B QUE - TSTI

1 (1200 lb.) beef
6 lb. salt
6 lb. brown sugar
2 lb. black pepper
Butchers paper

Masking tape
Mesquite wood (enough to fill pit)
Gunny (toe) sacks
Bailing wire

Cut dressed beef into large pieces about 10 to 12 pounds. Coat generously with above mixture of salt, brown sugar, and black pepper. Mix same ratio as many times as needed. Wrap coated beef in butchers paper very well and tape it up. Put into wet toe sacks. A couple of wrapped meat packages in each end of toe sack. Tie with bailing wire so you can get a hold of the sacks to remove from pit.

Dig pit 4 feet wide, 16 feet long, and 6 feet deep. We used this size for 1 (1200 pound) beef on foot. Early morning, fill pit with mesquite. Start fire, watching closely as not to start a fire elsewhere. Let coals burn down. Put meat on 24 hours before serving. Put meat in wet toe sacks into pit of coals; cover top of pit with sheets of tin and put dirt on top of tin so no smoke is coming out of pit. Let cook for 24 hours. Remove from pit.

PORK CHILI

2 lb. lean pork
1 Tbsp. meat tenderizer
2 Tbsp. chili powder
1 Tbsp. onion powder
1 can chicken broth

1 tsp. cumin
1 tsp. coriander
1 fresh bud garlic, chopped fine
¼ c. instant potatoes

Cut lean pork into bite-size pieces. Cover with water and boil for 30 minutes. Add seasonings and simmer for 1 hour. Keep tasting as strength of spices vary. Thicken with ¼ cup dry instant potatoes.

PORK CHOP SKILLET DINNER

6 lean pork chops
½ tsp. salt
¼ tsp. pepper
1 Tbsp. vegetable oil
½ tsp. savory leaves, crushed
½ bay leaf
2 c. tomato juice

½ c. water
1 small cabbage, cut into wedges
6 carrots, cut in 1 inch slices
1½ c. coarsely chopped onion
3 medium potatoes, peeled and
    quartered
¼ tsp. salt

Sprinkle chops with ½ teaspoon salt and pepper; brown in oil in a large iron skillet. Add savory, bay leaf, and tomato juice. Add ½ cup water; cover and simmer 30 minutes. Add remaining ingredients; cover and simmer 35 minutes or until vegetables are tender.

QUICK AND EASY MEXICAN CASSEROLE

2 lb. ground beef
5 oz. can evaporated milk
1 can Ro-Tel tomatoes (chop
    tomatoes but don't drain)

1 lb. Velveeta cheese, cubed
10 flour tortillas, torn in pieces

Brown ground beef and drain; add milk, tomatoes, and cheese. Simmer until cheese is nearly melted. Place ½ of flour tortillas in 9x9 inch square pan. Top with ½ of meat mixture. Repeat layers. Bake at 350° about 20 minutes or until hot.

RICE MEAT BALLS

1 c. Minute rice
1 lb. ground beef
1 slightly beaten egg
2 tsp. grated onion
2 tsp. salt

⅛ tsp. marjoram
Dash of pepper
½ c. tomato juice
½ c. sugar
2 c. tomato juice

Mix together lightly the rice, ground beef, egg, onion, salt, marjoram, pepper, and tomato juice. Shape into 18 balls. Place in skillet. Add sugar and 2 cups tomato juice. Bring to a boil, then cover and simmer 15 minutes, basting occasionally. This recipe is easy to add green pepper or other ingredients.

ROUND-UP WAGON STEW

3½ lb. chuck roast (rump or arm),
    cut in cubes
2 Tbsp. flour
2 Tbsp. fat
Tenderizer

1½ c. water
2 medium potatoes, cubed and
    parboiled
3 carrots, sliced
6 small onions, peeled

After preparing meat with tenderizer, dust beef cubes with flour. Heat fat in Dutch oven and brown meat in fat. Add water. Simmer over low heat for about 2 hours. Add vegetables during last 15 minutes and cook until tender. Serves 6.

SALMON PATTIES

1 can Honey Boy salmon
4 beaten eggs
1 tsp. onion powder
½ tsp. black pepper

½ c. water
30 saltine crackers, crumbled
1½ c. frozen diced hash brown
    potatoes (option)

Mix all ingredients and mix well. Add additional water if needed. Cover tightly and let set in refrigerator overnight. Heat grill or skillet with small amount of grease. Spoon onto grill desired size; flatten. Brown on 1 side and then turn. Serve hot with pepper sauce if desired. You can cook this immediately if you want to.

SCALLOPED POTATO CASSEROLE

2 lb. frozen hash brown potatoes
½ c. oleo
1 Tbsp. salt
¼ tsp. pepper
½ c. chopped onion

1 can cream of chicken soup
    (undiluted)
2 c. grated Cheddar cheese
2 c. or 2 (8 oz.) ctn. sour cream

Thaw potatoes (can shred real fine if you wish). Add all ingredients and put into a 3 quart casserole or 2 small ones. It can also be frozen. Crush 2 cups corn flakes and mix ¼ cup oleo and sprinkle on top. Bake at 350° for 45 minutes. Serves 10 to 12.

SHEPHERD'S BEEF PIE

4 c. cooked beef, cubed
2½ c. leftover gravy
2 or 3 c. leftover vegetables
    (potatoes, carrots, green beans,
    peas, etc.)

1 small onion, chopped
Salt and pepper
3 c. hot mashed potatoes
1 egg, well beaten

Combine meat, gravy, vegetables, onion, salt, and pepper. Heat to boiling point, stirring often. Put mixture in Dutch oven or baking dish. Combine mashed potatoes and egg in bowl; mix thoroughly. Cover top of casserole or drop in spoonfuls. Bake in hot oven at 425° for 15 or 20 minutes or until brown.

SLOPPY JOE MIX

20 lb. hamburger, browned and drained
2 medium onions, chopped
2½ tsp. pepper
4 Tbsp. salt
2 Tbsp. dry mustard
6 c. water
2 (42 oz.) bottles catsup
6 c. cracker crumbs (or 1 lb. box crackers)
2 Tbsp. soy sauce
2 Tbsp. Worcestershire sauce
2 bell peppers, chopped
¾ Tbsp. garlic powder
1 pkg. chili seasoning (or 8 oz. pkg. Morton's chili blend)

Brown and drain hamburger. Add 2 chopped onions. Use large roast pan. Add all other ingredients and cook until done.

SMOTHERED STEAK

1½ to 2 lb. steak, tenderized
Salt to taste
Pepper to taste

Cut steak into serving pieces; salt and pepper. Roll in flour and fry in hot oil, turning once until tender. Use iron skillet. Pour off oil and add a cup of water. Cover and cook on low about 1 hour. It makes its own gravy. Might need to add more water.

SUMMER SAUSAGE

2 lb. lean hamburger meat
¼ tsp. garlic powder
¼ tsp. onion salt
¼ tsp. mustard seed
2 Tbsp. liquid smoke
3 Tbsp. Morton's Tender-Quick meat cure
1 c. water

Mix well and make into 2 rolls. Wrap in foil (shinny side in). Chill for 24 hours. Seal foil on underside. Place on broiler pan and bake at least 90 minutes at 300°.

SUNDAY FRIED CHICKEN

1 frying chicken
Water
Crisco
Flour
Salt

Cut up fryer. Roll in flour. Dip in water and roll in flour again. Fry until golden brown.

TEXAS HASH

1 lb. ground beef
1 c. chopped onion
1 (No. 2) can tomatoes
1 c. green pepper, chopped
½ c. tomato soup

1 c. cooked rice
1 tsp. chili powder
Salt and pepper to taste
1 c. celery, chopped

Brown onions in bacon fat. Add meat; cook until pink is gone. Drain. Combine meat, onions, rice, vegetables, chili powder, salt, and pepper. Bake in a shallow casserole at 350° for 1 hour.

TOP HAND HASH

2 Tbsp. butter
¼ c. chopped onion
¼ c. chopped green pepper
1 lb. ground beef
1 tsp. salt
1 tsp. chili powder

¼ c. molasses
¼ c. prepared mustard
2 Tbsp. Worcestershire sauce
1 (16 oz.) can tomatoes
1 c. uncooked rice

Melt butter in iron skillet. Add onion and green pepper. Cook until onion is tender but don't brown. Add beef, salt, and chili powder. Brown beef, stirring with fork. While beef is browning, combine molasses and mustard. Stir in Worcestershire sauce. Add that and tomatoes to meat mixture. Add rice slowly. Cover and reduce heat. Simmer until rice is tender.

TURKEY AND DRESSING

Turkey
Salt
Butter
2 (10 inch) skillets corn bread
3 slices light bread
1 large onion, chopped
2 c. chopped celery
3 cans chicken broth

3 cans water
1 Tbsp. chicken bouillon
Ground sage
Poultry seasoning
Salt and pepper
⅛ tsp. cayenne pepper
6 boiled eggs, chopped
4 eggs, beaten

Remove neck and giblets. Wash turkey very well. Salt inside and out. Rub with softened butter. Place turkey breast down for more moist breast. Bake in covered roaster at 325° until done, time depending on size of bird.

Put small amount of oil in large pot. Add chopped onions until transparent. Add celery; cook a few minutes longer. Add broth, water, bouillon, crumbled corn bread, and sliced bread. Add more liquid if needed. Add spices to taste (brands differ in strength). Mash with potato masher. Add boiled eggs. Add beaten eggs. Stir well and bake at 350° for about 1 hour.

TURKEY GIBLET GRAVY

Turkey giblets
2 cans chicken broth
Turkey neck
Liquid from giblets and neck
3 boiled eggs, chopped
Salt

Pepper
Parsley flakes
2 Tbsp. cornstarch
1 c. water
Yellow food coloring

Cook turkey giblets (except liver) and neck until tender. Chop giblets. Remove meat from turkey neck. Add liquids. Bring to boil. Mix cornstarch in water and add to boiling mixture. Reduce heat. Add eggs, salt, and pepper to taste. Sprinkle parsley flakes. Color with yellow food coloring. May add more cornstarch if needed.

WESTERNER HASH

1 lb. ground beef
½ c. chopped bell pepper
½ c. chopped onion
½ tsp. basil
3½ c. canned tomatoes

½ c. uncooked rice
½ tsp. salt
Dash of pepper
American cheese slices

Brown onions, bell pepper, and beef in iron skillet. Add tomatoes, basil, rice, salt, and pepper. Cover and simmer for 25 minutes, stirring occasionally. Top with cheese slices and bake in 350° oven until cheese melts. Serve hot. *A great man pleaser.*

WAYNE'S FRITO CASSEROLE

1 large pkg. Fritos
1 large chopped onion

1 large can chili
½ lb. grated cheese

Spray casserole dish for easier cleaning. Place layer of Fritos on bottom of dish. Spread on layer of chili. Add layer of chopped onions, then layer of cheese. Add another layer of each. Top with small amount of Fritos. Bake in oven at 375° for 20 minutes.

Notes

Breads,

Rolls

MICROWAVE HINTS

1. Place an open box of hardened brown sugar in the microwave oven with 1 cup hot water. Microwave at high for 1½ to 2 minutes for ½ pound or 2 to 3 minutes for 1 pound.
2. Soften hard ice cream by microwaving at 30% power. One pint will take 15 to 30 seconds; one quart, 30 to 45 seconds; and one-half gallon, 45 seconds to one minute.
3. One stick of butter or margarine will soften in 1 minute when microwaved at 20% power.
4. Soften one 8-ounce package of cream cheese by microwaving at 30% power for 2 to 2½ minutes. One 3-ounce package of cream cheese will soften in 1½ to 2 minutes.
5. Thaw frozen orange juice right in the container. Remove the top metal lid. Place the opened container in the microwave and heat on high power 30 seconds for 6 ounces and 45 seconds for 12 ounces.
6. Thaw whipped topping...a 4½ ounce carton will thaw in 1 minute on the defrost setting. Whipped topping should be slightly firm in the center but it will blend well when stirred. Do not overthaw!
7. Soften jello that has set up too hard - perhaps you were to chill it until slightly thickened and forgot it. Heat on a low power setting for a very short time.
8. Dissolve gelatin in the microwave. Measure liquid in a measuring cup, add jello and heat. There will be less stirring to dissolve the gelatin.
9. Heat hot packs in a microwave oven. A wet fingertip towel will take about 25 seconds. It depends on the temperature of the water used to wet the towel.
10. To scald milk, cook 1 cup milk for 2-2½ minutes, stirring once each minute.
11. To make dry bread crumbs, cut 6 slices bread into ½-inch cubes. Microwave in 3-quart casserole 6-7 minutes, or until dry, stirring after 3 minutes. Crush in blender.
12. Refresh stale potato chips, crackers, or other snacks of such type by putting a plateful in the microwave oven for about 30-45 seconds. Let stand for 1 minute to crisp. Cereals can also be crisped.
13. Melt almond bark for candy or dipping pretzels. One pound will take about 2 minutes, stirring twice. If it hardens while dipping candy, microwave for a few seconds longer.
14. Nuts will be easier to shell if you place 2 cups of nuts in a 1-quart casserole with 1 cup of water. Cook for 4 to 5 minutes and the nut meats will slip out whole after cracking the shell.
15. When thawing hamburger meat, the outside will many times begin cooking before the meat is completely thawed. Defrost for 3 minutes, then remove the outside portions that have defrosted. Continue defrosting the hamburger, taking off the defrosted outside portions at short intervals.
16. To drain the fat from hamburger while it is cooking in the microwave oven (one pound cooks in 5 minutes on high), cook it in a plastic colander placed inside a casserole dish.
17. Cubed meat and chopped vegetables will cook more evenly if cut uniformly.
18. When baking large cakes, brownies, or moist bars, place a juice glass in the center of the baking dish to prevent a soggy middle and ensure uniform baking throughout.
19. Since cakes and quick breads rise higher in a microwave oven, fill pans just half full of batter.
20. For stamp collectors: Place a few drops of water on stamp to be removed from envelope. Heat in the microwave for 20 seconds and the stamp will come right off.
21. Using a round dish instead of a square one eliminates overcooked corners in baking cakes.
22. When preparing chicken in a dish, place meaty pieces around the edges and the bony pieces in the center of the dish.
23. Shaping meatloaf into a ring eliminates undercooked center. A glass set in the center of a dish can serve as the mold.
24. Treat fresh meat cuts for 15 to 20 seconds on high in the microwave oven. This cuts down on meat-spoiling types of bacteria.
25. A crusty coating of chopped walnuts surrounding many microwave-cooked cakes and quick breads enhances the looks and eating quality. Sprinkle a layer of medium finely chopped walnuts evenly onto the bottom and sides of a ring pan or Bundt cake pan. Pour in batter and microwave as recipe directs.
26. Do not salt foods on the surface as it causes dehydration (meats and vegetables) and toughens the food. Salt the meat after you remove it from the oven unless the recipe calls for using salt in the mixture.
27. Heat leftover custard and use it as frosting for a cake.
28. Melt marshmallow creme in the microwave oven. Half of a 7-ounce jar will melt in 35-40 seconds on high. Stir to blend.
29. Toast coconut in the microwave. Watch closely because it browns quickly once it begins to brown. Spread ½ cup coconut in a pie plate and cook for 3-4 minutes, stirring every 30 seconds after 2 minutes.
30. Place a cake dish up on another dish or on a roasting rack if you have difficulty getting the bottom of the cake done. This also works for potatoes and other foods that don't quite get done on the bottom.

BREADS, ROLLS

MATADOR COWBOYS REUNION

On the third Saturday in August every year the Matador Cowboys Reunion s held in Channing, Texas. Dick Shepherd helped form this organization along with he citizens of Channing. It started from the large Matador Ranch which sold out n the early 50's.

Dick started setting up his chuckwagon and cooking for the Ex-Matador cowboys and their families on Friday night before the big day of the reunion. Some of them brought bedrolls and some tepees and spent the night at the wagon.

This is when Sue and Jean started helping their dad cook on the chuck-wagon. At times he would be cooking for some ranch and they would go and help him some then.

After cooking the Friday night supper of the Matador Cowboys Reunion, Dick would hook up his mules to the wagon and pull it in the Parade on Saturday. He would take them to the Dalhart XIT Parade and to the Dumas Dogie Day Parade and a lot of other towns, too.

When Dick died in 1984, he left the chuckwagon to the 3 sons, Clyde, Red, and Frank. They didn't think they would ever be using it; they decided to sell it to Dee Parshbacker in Hayden, New Mexico, along with the mules, harness, and Hood Wagon all together. When it came time for the Matador Cowboys Reunion there was no chuckwagon to cook the usual Friday night supper. This had been done ever since the Reunion started in 1960. Dee came to Clyde and offered to loan the wagon back for the Reunion. The more the Shepherd's thought about it, the more they hated to see the chuckwagon out of the family. Dee knew it meant a lot to the family so offered to sell the chuckwagon back. Clyde, Sue, and Jean bought it.

The chuckwagon is kept in Ken and Sue's barn in Hartley, Texas. Ken, with the help of others, has set up the wagon and cooked Friday night of the Matador Cowboys Reunion ever since Dick died. Breakfast on Saturday and Sunday morning has been added.

Sue, edited by Jean

BANANA NUT BREAD

1¾ c. flour
1½ c. sugar
1 tsp. baking soda
½ tsp. salt
1 c. chopped pecans

2 eggs
⅓ c. buttermilk
1 tsp. vanilla
1 c. mashed bananas
½ c. butter

Preheat oven to 325°. Cream butter and sugar till lightly fluffy. Add 1 egg at a time, beating each well. Add flour, soda, salt, and buttermilk, then mix well. Fold in bananas, nuts, and vanilla. Bake in greased and floured loaf pan. Bake for 1 hour or until toothpick comes out clean.

BEER BREAD

3 c. flour
⅓ c. sugar
4 Tbsp. baking powder

1 tsp. salt
1 can beer (room temperature)
Butter

Mix flour, sugar, baking powder, and salt. Add beer. Pour into a greased loaf pan or muffin pans. Bake at 350° for 55 minutes in loaf pan. Brush top with butter when done.

CINNAMON PULL-APARTS

18 frozen rolls
1 small vanilla or butterscotch
    pudding (not instant)

1 tsp. cinnamon
½ c. butter or oleo
½ c. brown sugar

In the bottom of a greased Bundt pan, place frozen rolls. Sprinkle with pudding mix and cinnamon. Melt together butter and brown sugar; drizzle over rolls. Cover with towel and let rise all night. Bake at 350° for 30 minutes.

CHUCKWAGON DROP FRY BREAD

2 c. flour
2 tsp. baking powder
1 tsp. salt

2 Tbsp. sugar
2 Tbsp. oil

Mix all ingredients together. Add oil and very warm water; mix well. Let set 5 or 10 minutes and drop by spoonfuls into medium hot grease. Serve with honey or jam.

CORN BREAD DRESSING

4 pkg. corn bread mix
½ loaf bread or biscuits
1 pkg. celery, chopped
2 chopped onions
6 eggs
¾ lb. melted oleo
1 c. chopped pecans

3 tsp. salt
1 tsp. black pepper
5 tsp. sage
7 tsp. poultry seasoning
3 to 3½ qt. chicken broth or turkey broth

Crumble bread and let dry in a large pan or bowl. Saute onions and celery in oleo until tender. Pour into bread crumbs and mix. Add all other ingredients. Cook in a large pan about 1 hour or until done. Bake at 350°.

CORN BREAD DUTCH OVEN

1½ c. flour
1½ c. yellow corn meal
¼ c. sugar
1 tsp. salt
¼ tsp. soda

2 tsp. baking powder
1 beaten egg
1½ to 2 c. buttermilk
3 Tbsp. oil
14 inch Dutch oven

Mix flour, corn meal, sugar, salt, soda, and baking powder. Add buttermilk, small amount at a time, until it's thick cake batter consistency. Add beaten egg. Stir and add oil and stir. Spray Dutch oven with pan or nonstick spray. Not cowboy style but makes for easier cleaning. Pour small amount of oil in bottom of Dutch oven and bake with medium coals under oven and medium coals on top.

COWBOY CORN BREAD

2 lb. ground beef
1 small onion, diced
1 small can diced green chilies

1 lb. Cheddar cheese, grated
2 pkg. corn bread mix
1 can cream style corn

Cook ground beef with onion until done; drain. Add corn and chilies. Prepare corn bread mix. Drop ½ of batter into greased 9x13 inch pan. Spread evenly. Add ½ meat and corn mixture. Top with ½ of grated cheese. Repeat ½ corn bread mix, ½ meat, and corn mixture, adding remaining ½ of grated cheese on top. Bake at 350° for 30 minutes.

COWBOY HOT CAKES

2½ c. flour
1 Tbsp. baking powder
1 tsp. salt
¼ c. sugar

2 eggs, beaten
4 Tbsp. oil or shortening, melted
1½ c. milk (about)

Mix ingredients in order given. Add enough milk to make a fairly thin batter that pours with ease. Coat medium-hot griddle with oil; fry until bubbles surface. Turn and fry until golden brown. Makes about 2 dozen hot cakes.

DADDY'S SOURDOUGH STARTER

4 c. warm water
1 pkg. dry yeast
4 Tbsp. sugar
4 c. flour

1 potato, peeled and cut into
 fourths
1 (2 gal.) crock

Dissolve yeast in warm but not hot water. Let stand a few minutes. Add sugar; stir until dissolved. Start adding sifted flour, small amount at a time, until all flour is used. Mix well. Add potato. Cover with cup towel. Will be ready to use in 12 hours. Do not keep too cool. Stir occasionally.

After using 2 cups starter, add 1 cup warm water, 1 cup flour, and 1 tablespoon sugar.

DUTCH OVEN DOUGHNUTS

1 egg and 1 yolk
1 c. sugar
2 c. milk
½ tsp. salt

4 tsp. baking powder
¼ tsp. nutmeg
4 or 5 c. flour

Beat egg well and add sugar and milk. Sift salt, baking powder, and nutmeg; add flour together and add to mixture. Roll to ½ inch thickness. Cut with doughnut cutter and fry in deep hot oil. Drain on paper towels.

To prevent large cracks when frying, have the dough soft. Turn the cakes as they come to the top of the oil and often during the cooking. Too much flour makes dry, hard doughnuts.

EASY REFRIGERATOR ROLLS

2 pkg. yeast
2 c. very warm water (not hot)
½ c. sugar
2 tsp. salt

¼ c. soft shortening or butter
1 egg, beaten slightly with fork
6 c. flour

In large mixing bowl, dissolve yeast in water (sprinkle yeast into water and let set a few minutes). Add sugar, egg, salt, and shortening; stir. Add ½ of flour and stir in well. Stir in remaining flour; scrape into well greased bowl. Grease top of dough. Cover with Saran Wrap, then with tea towel and place in refrigerator. Rolls are easier to shape if dough is chilled. Make into rolls about 2 hours before needed and place in a warm place (to hasten rising, place pan of rolls over pan of warm water and cover with cloth). Bake at 425°.

FLOUR TORTILLAS

4 c. flour
⅛ tsp. baking powder
½ tsp. salt

½ c. shortening
1 c. hot water

Mix flour, baking powder, and salt in a bowl. Cut in shortening until well mixed. Add hot water. Work into a ball; knead on floured surface until smooth. Break off into balls the size of large walnuts. Roll into 6 to 8 inch rounds.

Cook on hot cast iron griddle. Turn when bubbles appear. Store wrapped in dish towel in a plastic bag. Tortillas take practice; don't be discouraged if they aren't round and soft the first few tries.

FRIED CORN BREAD

2 c. sifted corn meal

1 tsp. salt

Add enough hot water to make a stiff dough. Shape into 2 inch corn pones and fry in hot grease until brown. Serve at once.

JALAPENO CORN BREAD

2 eggs, well beaten
1 c. buttermilk
½ c. oil
1 can cream corn
1 medium onion, chopped
2 to 4 jalapeno peppers, chopped
  (seeds removed)
½ c. Cheddar cheese, grated

1 c. yellow corn meal
½ c. sifted flour
½ tsp. soda
1 tsp. salt
½ tsp. sugar
½ lb. hamburger or sausage,
  crumbled and browned

Combine eggs, buttermilk, oil, corn, onion, peppers, and cheese. Combine dry ingredients and add to egg mixture. Add meat. Stir until well blended. Pour into large iron skillet or a 13x15 inch pan. Bake for 35 to 40 minutes in a 425° oven.

QUICK MONKEY BREAD

½ c. chopped pecans
½ c. sugar
1 tsp. cinnamon

3 cans buttermilk biscuits
1 c. packed brown sugar
½ c. oleo, melted

Sprinkle chopped pecans evenly in the bottom of a well greased 10 inch Bundt pan; set aside. Combine sugar and cinnamon. Cut biscuits into quarters; roll each piece in sugar mixture and layer in pan. Combine brown sugar and oleo; pour over dough, also the rest of the cinnamon and sugar mixture. Bake at 350° for 30 to 40 minutes in pan; invert onto serving platter.

1615-94

MONKEY BREAD

2 c. warm water
1 pkg. yeast
½ c. sugar
2 eggs, beaten
3 c. flour

1 tsp. salt
4 Tbsp. oil
4 to 5 c. flour
½ c. butter, melted

Dissolve yeast in warm water. Add sugar. Add beaten eggs; mix well. Add 3 cups flour; mix well. Add salt and oil; mix well. Add flour and knead well. Let rise 1 hour. Pour melted butter into Bundt cake pan. Roll out dough ½ inch thick. Cut with biscuit cutter. Stand all biscuits on edge. Scrunch to fit in Bundt pan. Let rise 1 hour. Bake at 350° for 25 minutes.

THE COLLIE

When we lived at Turkey, Texas, we lived right on the highway and our pigs were always getting out. One day a stray collie dog came by and put the pigs back to the barn.

She must have traveled some distance as the bottoms of her feet were sore. When we fed her, she "adopted" us and we always called her "Collie."

When we moved to Channing, she rode in the front seat of the truck - along with Mother, Uncle Willis Garner, Sue, our cat, and myself.

Every Saturday when mother would get ready to kill the chickens for our Sunday dinner, she would point out the chickens she wanted and "Collie" would catch them and hold them down until Mother could get there.

She didn't like snakes and whenever she saw one of any kind, dead or alive, she would bark until it quit moving.

Jean, edited by Sue

MOTHER'S ANGEL BISCUITS

1 pkg. yeast
2 Tbsp. lukewarm water
5 to 5½ c. sifted flour
1 tsp. baking soda
3 tsp. baking powder

4 Tbsp. sugar
1 tsp. salt
1 c. shortening or oleo
2 c. buttermilk

Dissolve yeast in lukewarm water. Sift together dry ingredients; cut in shortening. Add yeast and buttermilk to dry mixture. Knead enough to hold together; roll dough to ½ to ¾ inch. Cut with biscuit cutter and fold in half. Bake at 400° for 15 to 20 minutes.

Note: Dough may be chilled before baking or frozen for later use.

NAVAJO FRY BREAD

3 c. flour
1 Tbsp. baking powder
1 Tbsp. sugar

1 tsp. salt
1¼ c. canned milk (about)
Lard or shortening (for frying)

Combine flour, baking powder, sugar, and salt. Add enough milk to make a soft dough. Turn out on floured board and knead. Pinch off a ball of dough big enough to pat out to a 9 inch flat cake. Heat lard or shortening in heavy iron skillet and test temperature by dropping in tiny pieces of dough. If pieces rise to top at once and begin to brown, the grease is ready. Fry dough until brown, then turn and brown other side.

PATSY'S CINNAMON ROLLS

2 c. warm water
⅔ c. sugar

5 tsp. yeast

Mix.

Add:

4 c. flour
2 eggs, beaten

⅓ c. melted shortening
1 Tbsp. salt

Mix well and add 2½ cups flour and mix until smooth. Put dough into well greased bowl. Let rest 20 minutes. Roll out on floured surface and add filling.

Sugar-Cinnamon Filling:

½ c. soft oleo
½ bag (2 lb.) brown sugar

3 Tbsp. cinnamon

Blend well (food processor does great) and spread onto dough; roll up into long roll and cut into slices. Put on oiled cookie sheet or sheet pan and let rise. Bake at 400° until brown. Top with icing.

ONE HOUR QUICK ROLLS

2 pkg. dry yeast
2 c. warm water
2 c. flour
1/3 c. Crisco oil

1/3 c. sugar
1 egg, beaten
2 tsp. salt
4 to 5 c. flour

Dissolve yeast in warm water. Add 2 cups flour, Crisco oil, sugar, egg, and salt, then stir. Add 4 to 5 cups flour. Let rise at least 25 minutes. Make into rolls; let rise a little while and bake at 400° for 15 to 20 minutes.

QUICK BISCUITS
(Dutch oven)

2 c. warm water
1 pkg. dry yeast
3 Tbsp. sugar
1 tsp. salt

2 tsp. baking powder
3 Tbsp. oil
2 1/2 to 3 c. flour
14 inch Dutch oven

Spray Dutch oven for easier cleaning. Add a little oil to bottom of Dutch oven. Dissolve yeast in warm water. Let stand a few minutes. Add sugar, salt, baking powder, and oil. Mix well. Add flour gradually; mix well. Pour out on floured board. Sprinkle flour on top. Pat out 1/2 inch thick and cut with biscuit cutter. Put in Dutch oven. Top with melted butter. Let rise until double. Bake in Dutch oven with coals on top and bottom.

QUICK STICKY BUNS

2 Tbsp. butter
1/4 c. brown sugar
1/4 c. pancake syrup
1/4 c. chopped nuts

1 tsp. cinnamon
1 pkg. (10 count) refrigerator
    biscuits

Combine the first 5 ingredients together in a layer cake pan. Top with the biscuits and bake as package directs or until golden brown. Remove from oven and turn out onto plate. Serves 4.

PINEAPPLE NUT BREAD

2 eggs, beaten
1/3 c. melted shortening
1 c. crushed pineapple (undrained)
1 c. chopped nuts
2 c. sifted flour

3 tsp. baking powder
1/3 c. sugar
1 tsp. salt
1 tsp. cinnamon

Mix dry ingredients and set aside. Beat eggs, shortening, and pineapple together. Add dry ingredients and mix well. Add nuts alternately with dry ingredients. Bake at 350° about 1 hour.

1615-94

PUMPKIN BREAD

2 c. sugar
1½ c. oil
5 eggs, beaten
2 c. pumpkin
2 c. flour
1½ tsp. cinnamon

1 tsp. salt
2 tsp. baking soda
1 tsp. nutmeg
2 small boxes coconut pie filling
(not instant)
1½ c. chopped pecans

Combine all ingredients together, mixing well. Bake in 2 large loaf pans at 350° for 45 to 60 minutes.

This bread is much better on the third day.

SAUSAGE CORN BREAD

1 c. flour
¾ tsp. soda
1 tsp. baking powder
1 large or 2 small eggs
½ to 1 lb. sausage

1 c. corn meal
¼ tsp. salt
2 Tbsp. sugar
1½ c. buttermilk

Sift dry ingredients together, then add eggs and buttermilk; mix well. Fry sausage; drain and crumble. Put sausage in the bottom of a lightly greased square pan. Pour batter over top and bake at 400° to 425° until lightly browned on top.

SOURDOUGH CINNAMON BISCUITS

2 c. starter
½ pkg. dry yeast
3 Tbsp. sugar
1 tsp. salt
3 tsp. baking powder

3 Tbsp. oil
2 c. flour
1 Tbsp. cinnamon
½ c. pecans

Add dry yeast to starter. Let set for 5 minutes. Add sugar, salt, baking powder, cinnamon, and oil; stir well. Add flour, a little at a time. Add pecans. Pour out on floured bowl and sprinkle flour on top. Pat down ½ inch thick. Cut with biscuit cutter. Place in 14 inch Dutch oven, that has been sprayed with Pam, and add 2 tablespoons oil to bottom of Dutch oven. Let rise till double. Bake with coals under and on top until brown on top and bottom.

SOURDOUGH CINNAMON ROLLS
(Dutch oven)

4 c. starter
1 pkg. dry yeast
1 tsp. salt
¼ c. sugar
3 to 4 c. flour

5 Tbsp. shortening
Melted butter
Cinnamon
Sugar

Add dry yeast to starter. Stir and let set 5 minutes. Add sugar, salt, and oil; mix well. Add sifted flour, small amount at a time. Pour out on floured board. Flour top and roll out in rectangle. Brush top with melted butter. Sprinkle cinnamon and sugar; roll up. Cut into slices 1 inch thick. Place in 16 inch Dutch oven that has been sprayed with Pam for easier cleaning. Add small amount of oil to bottom of oven. Bake with coals on top and bottom.

SOURDOUGH CORN BREAD

1 c. sourdough starter
Corn meal (enough to make a
    beatable batter)
1½ c. milk
2 Tbsp. sugar

2 eggs, beaten
½ tsp. salt
½ tsp. soda
¼ c. melted butter or oil

Mix starter, corn meal, milk, and eggs and stir thoroughly in large bowl. Stir in melted butter, salt, and soda. Turn into a 10 inch greased skillet or Dutch oven. Bake for 25 to 30 minutes.

SOURDOUGH PANCAKES

1 pkg. yeast
2 c. warm water
3 c. flour
2 eggs
½ c. sugar

½ tsp. salt
½ tsp. soda
1 tsp. vanilla
¼ c. oleo, melted

Mix yeast, warm water, and flour in a bowl with a lid. Let stand on the cabinet overnight, covered. Next morning, add eggs, sugar, salt, soda, vanilla, and melted oleo. Make into pancakes.

1615-94

SOURDOUGH BISCUITS
(Dutch oven)

1 (16 inch) Dutch oven
3 c. starter
3 Tbsp. sugar
2 tsp. salt

3 Tbsp. baking powder
5 Tbsp. oil
2½ to 3 c. flour

Spray Dutch oven for easier cleaning. Put small amount of oil in Dutch oven. To starter, add a little dry yeast. Let set a few minutes. Add sugar, salt, baking powder, and oil; mix well. Add flour gradually. Pour out onto floured board and add flour to top. Pat out with hand about ½ inch thick. Cut with biscuit cutter. Put in prepared Dutch oven. Top with melted butter. Let rise until double in size. Cook with coals on top and under Dutch oven.

THICK AND CHEWY PIZZA DOUGH

1 pkg. active dry yeast
1 c. lukewarm water

3 to 3¼ c. bread flour
1 tsp. salt

Dissolve the yeast in the lukewarm water. Combine 2½ cups of the flour and salt. Stir in yeast mixture. Knead the dough about 10 minutes, working in ½ to ¾ cup more flour so that the dough is still soft but no longer sticky. Put the dough in an oiled bowl; cover with plastic wrap and let rise until double in bulk, 40 to 60 minutes. Punch down the dough. Cover and let rise again until doubled, 45 to 60 minutes more. Punch down and let stand 10 minutes before shaping.

THIN CRUST PIZZA DOUGH

1 pkg. active dry yeast
1 c. lukewarm water

3 c. unbleached flour
1 tsp. salt

Dissolve yeast in water. Combine 2½ cups flour and salt. Stir in yeast mixture. Knead dough about 10 minutes, working up to ½ cup more flour so that the dough is still soft but not sticky. Put dough in an oiled bowl; cover with plastic wrap and let rise till double in bulk, 40 to 60 minutes. Punch down and let stand 10 minutes before shaping.

ZUCCHINI BREAD

3 eggs
2 c. sugar
1 c. oil
2 tsp. vanilla
2 c. grated zucchini squash
3 c. flour

1 tsp. soda
3 tsp. cinnamon
½ tsp. baking powder
1 tsp. salt
1 c. chopped pecans

Cream together eggs, sugar, oil, and vanilla. Add grated zucchini squash, flour, soda, cinnamon, baking powder, salt, and chopped pecans. Bake in 2 greased loaf pans for 1 hour at 350°.

Desserts

Common Baking Dishes and Pans

Spring Form Pan

Layer Cake or Pie Pan

Ring Mold

Baking or Square Pan

Loaf Pan

Brioche Pan

Angel Cake Pan

Bundt Tube

Equivalent Dishes

4-CUP BAKING DISH
= 9″ pie plate
= 8″ x $1^1 4$″ layer cake pan
= $7^3 8$″ x $3^5 8$″ x $2^1 4$″ loaf pan

6-CUP BAKING DISH
= 8″ or 9″ x $1^1 2$″ layer cake pan
= 10″ pie pan
= $8^1 2$″ x $3^5 8$″ x $2^5 8$″ loaf pan

8-CUP BAKING DISH
= 8″ x 8″ x 2″ square pan
= 11″ x 7″ x $1^1 2$″ baking pan
= 9″ x 5″ x 3″ loaf pan

10-CUP BAKING DISH
= 9″ x 9″ x 2″ square pan
= $11^3 4$″ x $7^1 2$″ x $1^3 4$″ baking pan
= 15″ x 10″ x 1″ flat jelly roll pan

12-CUP BAKING DISH OR MORE
= $13^1 2$″ x $8^1 2$″ x 2″ glass baking dish
= 13″ x 9″ x 2″ metal baking pan
= 14″ x $10^1 2$″ x $2^1 2$″ roasting pan

Total Volume of Pans

TUBE PANS

$7^1 2$″ x 3″ Bundt tube	6 cups
9″ x $3^1 2$″ fancy or Bundt tube	9 cups
9″ x $3^1 2$″ angel cake pan	12 cups
10″ x $3^3 4$″ Bundt tube	12 cups
9″ x $3^1 2$″ fancy tube mold	12 cups
10″ x 4″ fancy tube mold	16 cups
10″ x 4″ angel cake pan	18 cups

SPRING FORM PANS

8″ x 3″ pan	12 cups
9″ x 3″ pan	16 cups

RING MOLDS

$8^1 2$″ x $2^1 4$″ mold	$4^1 2$ cups
$9^1 4$″ x $2^3 4$″ mold	8 cups

BRIOCHE PAN

$9^1 2$″ x $3^1 4$″ pan	8 cups

DESSERTS

CHUCKWAGON COOK-OFFS

In the cook-offs, we enter as a team. We have from 2 to 6 people, depending on how many the rules allow. We go as a family, Jean, Sue, Ken, Peggy, and Clyde. A valued friend, Paul Askey, also helps us. We have won some outstanding awards in very tough competition and enjoy it all!

We enter from 3 to 6 cook-offs a year and have been in the winnings all except 2. We try to go to cook-offs close to home. Traveling gets expensive. In Texas, we have entered Amarillo, Abilene, Fritch, Lubbock, Midland, and Canyon, also Ruidoso, New Mexico. Most of them we entered several times in the last 5 years. I think the one we enjoyed winning the most was when we won First Overall in the Western Heritage Classic Chuck Wagon Cook-Off in Abilene in 1992. They only let you have 2 cooks, so the team decided it would be Sue and Jean. There were 24 chuck wagon teams participating. That was a thrill! It was the first time 2 women had ever won it.

In 1993 at the National Championship Chuck Wagon Cook-Off in Lubbock, we won First in meat, beans, bread, and dessert, all 4 foods. That was the first time that we know of, that all 4 foods were won by the same team.

In one cook-off we could only have 2 cooks so we (Sue and Jean) cooked on our wagon. Paul and Ken, who usually cook on our team, borrowed a wagon, entered the cook-off, and competed against us. We shared some Dutch ovens and cooking utensils with them since they didn't have very much. While Paul and Ken was setting up their camp we were setting up ours. We were digging our fire pit when Gary Morton, a Western Artist, a friend of ours, came by and "cowboylike" could hardly stand watching 2 women on the end of a shovel. He finished up the fire pit for us.

That cook-off was really fun. Us gals roped a first place trophy for vegetables. The guys "missed their loop" and came up with a big fat zero.

Sue, edited by Jean

AUNT BESSIE GARRISON'S APRICOT NECTAR POUND CAKE

1 c. Crisco
3 c. sugar
6 eggs
3 c. sifted flour
Dash of salt
¼ tsp. soda

1 c. or 8 oz. ctn. sour cream
½ c. apricot nectar
1 tsp. vanilla
1 tsp. orange extract
½ tsp. lemon, almond, or rum
    extract

Cream Crisco, sugar, and eggs. Stir in flour, salt, and soda. Add other ingredients. Cook in Bundt or angel food pan at 350° for 60 minutes.

Filling:

1 c. sugar
½ c. oleo

1 c. orange juice or apricot nectar

Bring to a rolling boil and pour over cake while hot. Wrap cake in aluminum foil for awhile. Freezes well.

BETTER THAN SEX CAKE

1 yellow cake mix
1 c. sugar
1 large pkg. vanilla instant pudding
    mix

1 (20 oz.) can crushed pineapple
1 c. coconut
1 small Cool Whip
1 c. chopped pecans

Bake the yellow cake mix in a 9x13 inch pan. While cake is baking, simmer pineapple with sugar. When cake is done, pour this over it, then sprinkle coconut on top. Let cake cool and mix 1 large package of instant vanilla pudding according to package directions and pour over cake. Put Cool Whip on top of the pudding. Sprinkle chopped pecans on top of that. Keep refrigerated.

BRANDY FRUIT CAKE

1 lb. candied cherries
¼ lb. English walnuts
¼ lb. pecan meats
½ lb. pitted dates
¼ lb. candied pineapple
¼ lb. preserved citron
½ lb. seeded raisins
¼ c. flour
1 c. shortening

½ c. sugar
½ c. honey
5 well beaten eggs
1½ c. flour
1 tsp. salt
1 tsp. baking powder
1 tsp. allspice
½ tsp. cloves
¼ c. orange or grape juice

Halve cherries, nuts, and dates. Cut pineapple and citron the size of almonds. Roll fruit in ¼ cup flour. Cream shortening and sugar. Add honey, then eggs and beat well. Add flour sifted with dry ingredients alternately with fruit juice. Beat thoroughly. Pour batter over floured fruits and mix well.

Line loaf pan or angel food pan with brown paper. Grease, then line with waxed paper. Grease, then line again with waxed paper. Grease again. Pour in mixture. Do not flatten. Bake in slow oven (250°) 3 to 4 hours. Place pan with 2 to 3 cups of water under cake. When cooled, pour brandy over cake and wrap in brandy soaked rag. Add brandy whenever. Store in cool place.

CAKE THAT NEVER LASTS

3 c. flour
1 tsp. cinnamon
1 tsp. soda
1 tsp. salt
2 c. sugar
1¼ c. cooking oil

1 (8 oz.) can crushed pineapple
    with juice
1½ tsp. vanilla
3 eggs
2 c. diced ripe bananas
1 c. chopped pecans

Sift together into a large mixing bowl the flour, cinnamon, soda, salt, and sugar, then add the cooking oil, pineapple, vanilla, eggs, bananas, and pecans. Mix all together but do not beat. Pour into 9 inch greased Bundt or tube pan. Bake at 350° for 1 hour and 20 minutes. Cool before removing from the pan.

CAKE YOU DON'T FROST

1½ c. sugar
½ c. margarine
½ c. Crisco
3 mashed bananas
2 eggs, beaten
1 tsp. soda
½ tsp. salt

2 c. flour
¼ c. milk
1 tsp. vanilla
½ c. margarine
1 c. brown sugar
1 c. pecans
1 c. coconut

Combine sugar, margarine, and Crisco. Add bananas, eggs, and vanilla; mix well. Sift flour, soda, and salt; add to mixture and mix well. Pour into 9x13 inch greased and floured pan. Mix margarine, pecans, brown sugar, and coconut together; add to top of unbaked cake. Bake at 350° for 30 to 40 minutes.

CARROT CAKE

2 c. sugar
4 eggs
2 tsp. soda
⅓ c. buttermilk
1½ c. Crisco oil

3 c. flour
2 tsp. cinnamon
1 c. chopped pecans
3 c. grated carrots
1 tsp. lemon extract

Cream sugar, eggs, and Crisco oil. Into mixture, blend flour, soda, buttermilk, and cinnamon. Stir in pecans, carrots, and lemon extract, mixing well. Bake in tube pan or 2 loaf pans at 300° for 1½ hours. Cool. Cover with glaze of 1 cup powdered sugar and orange juice to spread.

CHOCOLATE CAKE

3 c. flour
⅔ c. cocoa
1 tsp. soda
1¼ tsp. baking powder
1 tsp. salt
½ c. shortening

2 c. sugar
2 eggs, beaten
1 tsp. vanilla
2 c. liquid sour cream or sour milk,
    water, or buttermilk

Sift flour and then measure. Sift again with cocoa, soda, baking powder, and salt. Work shortening with spoon until soft. Gradually add sugar. Beat until fluffy. Add eggs; blend well and add flour mixture with liquid and vanilla. Bake at 350° for 30 to 35 minutes. Cool and frost.

CHOCOLATE POUND CAKE

1 c. butter or margarine
½ c. shortening
3 c. sugar
5 eggs
1 tsp. vanilla extract

3 c. flour
½ tsp. baking powder
½ tsp. salt
4 Tbsp. cocoa
1 c. milk

Cream together butter and shortening. Add sugar and mix well. Add eggs, 1 at a time, beating after each addition. Add vanilla. Combine dry ingredients and add alternately with milk to creamed mixture. Bake in a greased 10 inch tube pan at 325° for 80 minutes.

DUMP CAKE

1 (20 oz.) can cherry pie filling
1 (8¼ oz.) can crushed pineapple
1 pkg. yellow cake mix

1 c. margarine, melted
1 (3½ oz.) can flaked coconut
1 c. chopped pecans

Spoon pie mix in bottom of 9x13 inch pan. Spread pineapple over pie filling. Sprinkle dry cake mix over pineapple. Pour melted margarine evenly over all. Sprinkle with coconut and pecans. Bake at 325° for 1 hour. It might take a little longer.

FRUIT COCKTAIL CAKE

2 c. flour
1½ c. sugar
2 tsp. soda
½ tsp. salt

1 can fruit cocktail
2 eggs
1 c. chopped nuts
¼ c. brown sugar

Sift together flour, sugar, soda, and salt. Add cocktail and eggs; mix well and add nuts. Pour into 9x13 inch greased pan. Sprinkle top of cake with brown sugar. Bake at 325° for 45 to 55 minutes.

Icing:

1 c. oleo
1 c. canned milk
1 c. sugar

1 tsp. vanilla
1 c. coconut

Boil oleo, milk, and sugar for 8 minutes after sugar and oleo melts. Add vanilla and coconut; beat until thick. Ice cake while warm.

EARTHQUAKE CAKE

1½ c. chopped pecans
1½ c. coconut
1 pkg. German chocolate cake mix
   (as directed)

1 (8 oz.) cream cheese
½ c. oleo
1 lb. powdered sugar

Spread pecans and coconut in a greased 9x13 inch pan. Pour in prepared cake mix. Soften and cream the oleo, cream cheese, and powdered sugar in microwave; pour over cake mix. Bake as directed on cake mix, then bake 10 to 15 minutes longer.

GERMAN CHOCOLATE CAKE

2 c. sugar
1 c. buttermilk
¼ tsp. salt
4 egg yolks
1 tsp. vanilla
1 pkg. German's sweet chocolate,
   melted in ½ c. hot water

1 c. Crisco
2½ c. flour
1 tsp. soda
4 egg whites, beaten stiff

Line 3 (8 or 9 inch) round cake pans with 1 layer of brown paper bag and 2 layers of waxed paper; trim excess over edge of pans.

Dissolve soda in ¼ cup buttermilk. Mix Crisco, sugar, and egg yolks, then remaining buttermilk and then soda mixture. Add sifted flour and salt; alternate with chocolate mixture. Fold in egg whites and vanilla. Bake at 350° until toothpick comes out clean when stuck in center of cake.

German Chocolate Cake Icing:

3 egg yolks
1½ c. sugar
2 Tbsp. flour
1½ c. canned milk

½ c. margarine
1¼ c. chopped pecans
1¼ c. coconut
1 tsp. vanilla

Mix flour and sugar together and add milk, beaten egg yolks, and margarine; cook until thick. Remove from heat. Add vanilla, pecans, and coconut. Ice top and sides of cake.

GERMAN CHOCOLATE POUND CAKE

2 c. sugar
1 c. shortening
4 eggs
2 tsp. vanilla
2 tsp. butter flavoring

1 c. buttermilk
3 c. sifted flour
½ tsp. soda
1 tsp. salt
1 pkg. German's sweet chocolate

Cream sugar and shortening. Add eggs, vanilla, butter flavoring, and buttermilk. Sift together flour, soda, and salt; add. Mix well, then add German's chocolate that has been softened in warm oven or in double boiler. Blend together well. Bake in 9 inch stem pan or 10 inch Bundt pan that has been well greased and dusted with flour, about 1½ hours at 300° or until toothpick inserted in the center comes out clean. Remove cake from pan while still hot and place under a tight fitting cake cover; leave covered until cold.

LEMON PECAN CAKE

1 lb. brown sugar
1 lb. oleo
6 eggs
4 c. flour

2 oz. lemon extract
½ lb. candied cherries
½ lb. candied pineapple
1 lb. pecans

Mix and bake in loaf pan in slow oven at 250° for 2½ to 3 hours, when top is cracked or brown. Bake with pan of water underneath.

PINA COLADA CAKE

1 box yellow cake mix
½ Tbsp. pineapple flavoring

½ Tbsp. coconut flavoring

Mix cake as directed on box. Add flavorings. Bake as directed. Use 2 layer pans (8 or 9 inch pans).
Frosting:

1½ oz. cream cheese
½ Tbsp. butter
½ tsp. vanilla
1½ c. powdered sugar
4 oz. Cool Whip

1 small can crushed pineapple
Toasted coconut
Maraschino cherries, chopped
Chopped pecans

Cream first 3 ingredients; add sugar gradually. Mix until creamy. Add Cool Whip. Fold in pineapple. Frost cake. Sprinkle coconut, cherries, and pecans over each layer. Top with whole cherries. Keep refrigerated.

PINEAPPLE CAKE

2 c. flour
2 tsp. soda
½ tsp. salt
1 (No. 2) can crushed pineapple

1½ c. sugar
2 tsp. vanilla
2 eggs

Icing:

1 c. sugar
1 can evaporated milk

½ c. butter
1 c. coconut

Mix all ingredients with pineapple juice and all. Mix all at once in a bowl and beat. Bake in oblong pan 25 or 30 minutes at 350°.

Icing: Mix sugar, milk, and butter in saucepan. Bring to boil. Cook 2 minutes. When cake is done, sprinkle coconut over cake. Pour icing over cake.

PINEAPPLE ORANGE CAKE

1 butter cake mix
1 can mandarin oranges (juice too)

½ c. Wesson oil
3 eggs

Mix all together and beat 2 minutes. Pour into 3 greased and floured pans. Bake at 350° for 20 to 30 minutes.

Frosting:

1 large can crushed pineapple
1 large Cool Whip

1 large instant pudding mix (vanilla)

Put pineapple in large mixing bowl. Add pudding mix, then fold in Cool Whip. Frost cake and refrigerate.

PINEAPPLE UPSIDE-DOWN CAKE

1 pkg. yellow cake mix
¼ c. butter or margarine
½ c. brown sugar

Pineapple slices
Maraschino cherries

Prepare cake mix according to package directions. Melt butter in skillet at 220°. Add sugar. Arrange fruit in butter-sugar mixture. Pour cake batter over fruit. Cover skillet; bake at 220° for 50 minutes. Turn cake out on plate immediately.

PRUNE CAKE

1½ c. sugar
3 eggs
1 c. sour milk
1 tsp. soda
2 c. flour
1 tsp. ground cloves

1 tsp. cinnamon
½ tsp. salt
1 c. unsweetened cooked prunes
1 c. chopped pecans
1 tsp. vanilla
1 c. Crisco oil

Cream sugar and eggs. Add soda to milk. Add flour and spices alternately with milk. Add prunes, nuts, and vanilla. Add oil last and bake at 350° in a greased loaf pan or in layers. Bake about 1 hour.

Icing:

1 c. brown sugar
⅓ c. cream

5 Tbsp. butter
1 tsp. vanilla

Bring to a boil. Cook for 3 minutes. Let cool and thicken (with powdered sugar if necessary). Spread on cake.

PUMPKIN CAKE

1 box yellow cake mix
2 tsp. pumpkin pie spice
1 small pkg. vanilla instant pudding
    mix
1 tsp. cinnamon

1 c. canned pumpkin
⅓ c. oil
3 eggs
½ c. water

Mix all dry ingredients together well. Add other ingredients. Grease and lightly flour Bundt cake pan; pour in mixture. Bake at 325° for 1 hour. Cool completely before taking out of pan.

Glaze:

1 c. powdered sugar
¼ tsp. pumpkin pie spice

1 to 2 Tbsp. water

Mix glaze and drizzle over the top of cake. Real moist cake!

RUM CAKE

Before you start, sample the rum and check quality. Good isn't it? Now, go ahead. Select a large mixing bowl, measuring cups, and check that rum again for quality. It must be just right ... try it again.

With an electric beater, beat 1 cup butter in a large fluffy bowl. Add 1 teaspoon sugar and beat it again. Meanwhile, make certain that the rum is of the best quality. Add 2 large eggs, 2 cups fried fruit. Beat until very high. If fruit gets stuck in beaters, pry out with a screwdriver. Sample rum again to check for consistency.

Next, sift 3 cups baking powder; add pinch of rum, 1 teaspoon soda, 1 cup pepper (or maybe salt??). Anyhow, don't fret, just taste the rum again ... *Zowie!!* Next, sift in ½ pint lemon juice; fold in chopped buttermilk, and add strained nuts. Sample rum again.

Now ... 1 tablespoon brown sugar or whatever color is around; mix well. Grease oven and turn on cake pan to 350°. Now pour the whole mess into the oven and ... (oops, where did I put that mop?). In second thought, and also third and fourth, forget the oven, forget the cake ... check the rest of the rum and go to bed.

RUSTY'S RED VELVET CAKE

1½ c. sugar
½ c. Crisco
2 eggs
1 tsp. vanilla
1 tsp. butter flavoring
2 oz. red food coloring

5 Tbsp. cocoa
2½ c. flour
1 c. buttermilk
1 tsp. salt
1 Tbsp. vinegar
1 tsp. soda

First line 3 (8 inch) round cake pans with 1 liner of brown paper sack and 2 layers of waxed paper. Just put the brown paper and waxed paper in cake pan and push down with another cake pan.

Cream Crisco, sugar, eggs, vanilla, and butter flavoring. Make paste of cocoa and red food coloring. Add to Crisco mixture. Add salt to flour in sifter. Alternate, adding flour and buttermilk to first mixture. In small bowl, mix soda and vinegar. Add to batter and blend. Bake at 350°. Don't get too done. Cool and ice with following.

Rusty's Red Velvet Cake Icing:

5 Tbsp. flour
½ tsp. salt
1½ c. milk
1½ c. Crisco

1½ c. sugar
2 tsp. vanilla
¼ tsp. butter flavoring

Cook milk, flour, and salt until thick, stirring constantly. *Let cool.* Cream Crisco and sugar very well. Add vanilla and butter flavoring. Combine with first mixture. Beat well and put between layers and on top and sides. Cake should be moist.

Rusty won awards with this cake in 4-H.

SOURDOUGH APPLESAUCE CAKE

Mix, cover, and let stand while you mix the rest:

1 c. sourdough starter
¾ c. nonfat dry milk
1 c. flour

1½ c. applesauce
½ c. raisins (optional)

Cream together:

½ c. shortening
½ c. white sugar

½ c. brown sugar

Add and beat well:

1 egg
½ tsp. salt
1 tsp. cinnamon
½ tsp. nutmeg

½ tsp. allspice
½ tsp. cloves
2 tsp. soda
½ c. chopped nuts

Combine with sourdough mixture and beat by hand. Bake at 325° until done.

SOURDOUGH CHOCOLATE CAKE

Mix the following and let stand for at least 3 hours in a warm place:

½ c. sourdough starter	¾ c. dry milk granules
1 c. warm water	6 Tbsp. cocoa
1½ c. flour	

Cream together:

1 c. sugar	½ tsp. salt
¾ c. shortening	1 tsp. vanilla

Add 2 eggs; beat well after each, and 1½ teaspoons soda, dissolved in 2 tablespoons warm water. Combine with sourdough mixture and beat by hand. Makes 3 (9 inch) layers. Bake at 325° for 25 to 30 minutes.

STRAWBERRY POUND CAKE

1 white cake mix	½ (8 oz.) thawed strawberries
1 small box strawberry Jell-O	1 lb. box powdered sugars
3 Tbsp. flour	¼ c. butter, melted
½ c. water	½ (8 oz.) box frozen (thawed)
1 c. Wesson oil	strawberries
4 eggs, separated	

Mix in order given. Beat in egg yolks, 1 at a time. Fold in beaten egg whites. Bake in 13x9x2 inch greased and floured cake pan at 350° for 40 minutes.

Icing: Mix powdered sugar, butter, and strawberries together. Pour over cake.

STRAWBERRY THING

1 pkg. strawberry Jell-O	1 angel food cake
2 c. hot water	1 container Cool Whip
1 pkg. frozen strawberries	

Place angel food cake in bowl, which has tight lid (Tupperware). Mix Jell-O in boiling water to dissolve. Add strawberries and mix. Pour Jell-O mixture over cake. Put on lid. Do not bump (cake will explode). Put in refrigerator and chill. Can chill overnight. Top with Cool Whip.

TWENTY MINUTE FUDGE CAKE

2 c. sugar
2 c. flour
½ c. oleo
½ c. shortening
4 Tbsp. cocoa

1 c. water
½ c. buttermilk
2 eggs, slightly beaten
1 tsp. soda
1 tsp. vanilla

Icing:

½ c. oleo
4 Tbsp. cocoa
6 Tbsp. milk

1 lb. powdered sugar
1 tsp. vanilla
1 c. chopped pecans

Sift together sugar and flour. Mix in saucepan the oleo, shortening, cocoa, and water. Bring to a rapid boil and pour over dry ingredients; mix well. Add buttermilk, eggs, soda, and vanilla. Mix well and pour into a greased pan. Bake 25 minutes at 400°.

Icing: Start 5 minutes before cake is done. Melt and bring to a boil the oleo, cocoa, and milk. Add powdered sugar, vanilla, and pecans; mix well. Spread on cake immediately.

TEXAS PECAN CAKE AND GLAZE

6 Tbsp. butter
1 c. sugar
1 egg
½ tsp. vanilla
1½ c. flour

1 tsp. baking soda
½ tsp. salt
½ c. milk
½ c. sourdough starter

Beat butter, sugar, egg, and vanilla together until fluffy. Mix flour, baking soda, and salt together; add alternately with sourdough starter, blending after each addition. Blend in milk. Pour into sprayed tube or Bundt cake pan. Bake at 350° for 35 minutes. Remove from pan and cool.

Glaze:

¾ c. brown sugar
¼ tsp. salt
6 Tbsp. cornstarch

2 Tbsp. butter
¾ c. water

Combine sugar, cornstarch, and salt in saucepan. Stir in water; cook, stirring constantly, until mixture thickens and boils. Boil 1 minute. Add butter. Cool mixture until spreadable. Cover with whole pecan halves.

TEXAS FUDGE CAKE

2 c. flour
2 c. sugar
½ c. oleo
½ c. shortening
1 c. water

3½ Tbsp. cocoa
½ c. buttermilk
1 tsp. soda
2 eggs
1 tsp. vanilla

Put flour and sugar in mixing bowl and set aside. Now put oleo, shortening, water, and cocoa in a pan; bring to a boil. Add sugar and flour mixture. Add buttermilk, soda, eggs, and vanilla. Mix all together and pour into 10x15 inch greased and floured baking pan. Bake 20 minutes at 400°.

Frosting:

½ c. oleo, melted
4 Tbsp. cocoa

4 to 5 Tbsp. milk
1 lb. confectioners sugar

Mix and spread over cake.

FUDGE ICING

1 c. sugar
¼ c. cocoa
½ c. oleo
½ c. milk

2 Tbsp. Karo
1 lb. powdered sugar
1 tsp. vanilla
1 c. chopped nuts (optional)

Stir sugar, cocoa, oleo, milk, and Karo. Boil 3 minutes, then cool. Add powdered sugar and vanilla. Add nuts if you like.

MOTHER'S CARAMEL ICING

2 c. sugar (white)
¼ c. margarine

1 tsp. salt
1 c. milk

Melt white sugar in cast iron skillet. Best not to stir until melted; use low heat. When sugar is dissolved, stir and add margarine, milk, and salt. It will scare you but just keep stirring over heat until the chunks are dissolved. Pour over cake. Best to use oblong cake in the pan.

If Mother browned her sugar a little too much, it was then called Burnt Sugar Icing.

QUICK CARAMEL FROSTING

¼ c. butter
¾ c. brown sugar

3 Tbsp. milk
2 c. sifted powdered sugar

Melt butter in saucepan and stir in brown sugar. Cook over low heat for 2 minutes. Add milk and bring to a full boil. Cool to lukewarm without stirring. Add powdered sugar and beat until smooth.

BEEF BROWNIES

¼ lb. ground beef
3 eggs
1 c. sugar
½ tsp. salt
1 tsp. vanilla

½ c. butter, softened
2 sq. chocolate, melted
¾ c. flour
½ tsp. baking powder
1 c. nuts, chopped

Cook beef until it is brown and crumbles. Drain off all grease. Beat together eggs, sugar, salt, vanilla, butter, and chocolate. Add beef and dry ingredients. Add nuts. Spread in 9x9 inch pan. Bake 35 minutes at 350°. Cool; sprinkle with powdered sugar, if desired, and cut into squares.

They're so moist and delicious they're unreal.

BROWNIES

2 c. sugar
1 c. flour
3 Tbsp. cocoa
½ c. butter

2 beaten eggs
2 tsp. vanilla
½ tsp. salt
1 c. chopped pecans

Cream sugar and butter. Add eggs. Sift flour and cocoa together. Add flour, salt, and then vanilla and nuts. Bake in 8x8 inch square pan at 350°.

BUTTER NUT CHEWIES

½ c. melted butter flavor Crisco
2 eggs
2 c. firmly packed light brown sugar
1 tsp. vanilla

1½ c. unsifted flour
2 tsp. baking powder
½ tsp. salt
1 c. chopped nuts

Preheat oven to 350°. Grease 13x9x2 inch pan. Beat eggs until light and foamy in large bowl of electric mixer. Beat in sugar, vanilla, and Crisco until creamy. Combine flour with baking powder and salt. Add to egg mixture. Mix at low speed until blended. Stir in nuts at low speed (mixture will be stiff). Spread evenly in prepared pan. Bake at 350° for 25 to 30 minutes or until top is lightly browned. Cool 10 to 15 minutes. Cut into bars. Makes 2 dozen.

Justin Wells ©94

CHERRY CRISP

⅓ c. flour
¾ c. rolled oats
⅓ c. margarine
⅔ c. sugar
1½ Tbsp. corn starch

1 (16 oz.) can pitted sour cherries
⅛ tsp. cinnamon
⅛ tsp. nutmeg
1 Tbsp. lemon juice

Combine the flour and rolled oats. Cut in margarine until the mixture is crumbly; mix in ⅓ cup of the sugar. Set aside for topping.

Drain the cherries, reserving the juice. Combine the remaining sugar with the corn starch, spices, and lemon juice. Slowly blend in the cherry juice. Cook over low heat, stirring constantly, until the sauce is thick and clear. Add the cherries. Pour into a greased 8 inch square baking pan. Sprinkle with topping. Bake at 375° for 30 minutes.

CONFETTI HOLIDAY ROUNDS

1 c. butter, softened
½ c. confectioners sugar
1 tsp. vanilla
2 c. all-purpose flour

½ tsp. salt
½ c. chopped pecans
¼ c. chopped red glace cherries
¼ c. chopped green glace cherries

Beat together butter and sugar until creamy and fluffy. Add vanilla. Gradually stir in flour, mixing thoroughly. Stir in pecans and cherries. Using rounded teaspoonfuls of dough, shape into balls. Place on ungreased cookie sheet and flatten. Bake in preheated 350° oven 10 to 12 minutes or until lightly browned. Remove from cookie sheets and cool completely. Makes about 4 dozen.

COUNTRY LEMON SQUARES

Crust:

2 c. flour
¼ c. sugar
½ tsp. salt

½ c. melted butter
½ c. finely chopped pecans

Filling:

6 eggs
2 c. sugar
2 Tbsp. flour
6 Tbsp. lemon juice

1 Tbsp. grated lemon peel
(optional)
Powdered sugar

Prepare oven to 350°. Grease a 13x9x2 inch baking pan. To prepare crust, combine flour, sugar, salt, and butter in mixing bowl; blend with electric mixer on medium speed until mixture resembles corn meal. Stir in pecans. Press firmly and evenly into prepared pan. Bake 20 minutes or until very light golden brown.

To prepared filling, combine eggs, sugar, flour, lemon juice, and peel in mixing bowl; stir until smooth. Pour into baked crust. Bake 20 to 25 minutes or until filling is set. Cool completely on wire rack. Dust lightly with powdered sugar. Store, covered, in refrigerator. Makes 15 to 18 servings.

COWBOY COOKIES

1 c. shortening
1 c. sugar
1 c. brown sugar
2 eggs
1 tsp. vanilla
2 c. flour

1 tsp. soda
½ tsp. baking powder
½ tsp. salt
2 c. oats
1 (6 oz.) pkg. chocolate chips
1 c. coconut

Cream shortening and sugars together until light and fluffy. Stir in eggs and vanilla. Sift together flour, soda, baking powder, and salt; add to creamed mixture. Add oats, mixing well. Stir in chocolate chips and coconut. Drop by teaspoon onto greased cookie sheet. Bake at 350° for 7 to 9 minutes.

COW CHIP COOKIES

2 c. brown sugar
6 eggs
2 c. white sugar
1 c. melted oleo

1 tsp. vanilla
1 tsp. syrup
4 tsp. soda

Mix above, then add ½ pound peanut butter and mix well.

Add:

1 (22 oz.) box quick cooking
    oatmeal

½ lb. chocolate chips
½ lb. M&M's

Add 1 cup chopped pecans; mix well. Drop on cookie sheet by teaspoon. Bake at 350° for 10 to 12 minutes. No flour in the recipe. This makes a large batch.

GRANDMA SHEPHERD'S OLD-FASHIONED TEA CAKES

1 c. sugar
½ c. lard (or Crisco)
1 egg
1 tsp. vanilla
1 tsp. nutmeg (optional)

1 tsp. baking powder
½ tsp. soda
½ tsp. salt
3 c. flour
½ c. sour milk (or buttermilk)

Mix sugar, lard, eggs, and vanilla together. Sift flour, baking powder, soda, and salt together, then add alternately with milk. Roll out on floured board and cut with a biscuit cutter. Bake on greased cookie sheet at about 315° for 10 to 12 minutes.

NO BAKE COOKIES

1½ qt. sugar
4 Tbsp. cocoa
1½ c. milk
1½ c. oleo

1½ c. chunky peanut butter
2¼ qt. rolled oats
½ Tbsp. vanilla

1. Stir first 4 ingredients over low heat until butter is melted.
2. Bring to a boil and boil for 1 or 2 minutes.
3. Add next 3 ingredients.
4. Mix together and drop by spoon on waxed paper.

NUT ROLL DOUGH

½ lb. margarine
4 c. flour
2 Tbsp. sugar
½ tsp. salt

3 egg yolks
3 pkg. dry yeast
¼ c. cold milk

Sift flour and cut in margarine until fine crumbs. Add rest of ingredients and work dough until it leaves the sides of the bowl. Roll dough out in small pieces on granulated sugar. Cut into small squares and put your filling on with a knife. Roll up and place close together on cookie sheet and bake at 350° until brown.

Nut Roll Filling:

1 lb. ground nuts
¼ c. milk

2 Tbsp. melted butter
1 c. sugar

Melt butter and cool. Add nuts, milk, and sugar; mix. If too dry, add milk to make moist enough to spread.

PEANUT BUTTER COOKIES

½ c. butter
½ c. peanut butter
½ c. sugar
1¼ c. flour
1½ c. brown sugar

1 egg
¾ tsp. soda
½ tsp. baking powder
¼ tsp. salt

Cream butter, peanut butter, sugar, and egg. Add sifted dry ingredients. Drop by spoonful and flatten on greased cookie sheet. Bake at 375° for 10 to 12 minutes.

PECAN KRISPIES

½ c. shortening
½ c. butter
2½ c. brown sugar
2 beaten eggs

2½ c. flour
¼ tsp. salt
½ tsp. soda
1 c. chopped pecans

Thoroughly cream shortening, butter, and sugar; add eggs and beat well. Add flour, sifted with salt and soda. Add pecans. Drop from teaspoon onto greased cookie sheet. Bake at 350° for 15 to 17 minutes and remove from sheet immediately.

PEGGY'S WHOLE WHEAT BROWNIES

2 c. sugar
½ c. whole wheat flour
1 c. all-purpose flour
½ c. cocoa

1 c. melted oleo
4 eggs
2 tsp. vanilla
½ c. chopped pecans

Measure and sift together the dry ingredients. Add melted oleo, eggs, and vanilla. Beat until smooth. Fold in pecans. Pour into greased 9x13 inch pan. Bake 25 minutes at 350°.

PUMPKIN CHEESE ROLL

3 eggs
1 c. sugar
⅔ c. pumpkin
1 tsp. lemon juice
¾ c. flour
1 tsp. baking powder
2 tsp. cinnamon
1 tsp. ginger

½ tsp. nutmeg
½ tsp. salt
1 c. chopped pecans
1 c. powdered sugar
2 (3 oz.) pkg. cream cheese
4 Tbsp. margarine
½ tsp. vanilla

Beat eggs for 5 minutes. Gradually beat in sugar. Stir in pumpkin and add lemon juice. In another bowl, mix flour, baking powder, cinnamon, ginger, nutmeg, and salt. Fold dry ingredients into pumpkin mixture and spread into greased and floured 15x10x1 inch cookie sheet. Top with chopped nuts. Bake at 375° for 15 minutes.

Sprinkle towel with powdered sugar; turn cake onto towel. Sprinkle again with powdered sugar. Roll and cool for 1 hour. Mix powdered sugar, cream cheese, margarine, and vanilla. Unroll cake. Spread in mixture and roll again. Can be frozen.

RANGER COOKIES

1 c. shortening
1 c. brown sugar
1 c. white sugar
2 c. corn flakes
2 c. oatmeal
2 eggs
2 c. flour

2 tsp. soda
1 tsp. baking powder
1/2 tsp. salt
1 c. coconut
1 tsp. vanilla
1 c. chopped pecans

Cream shortening. Add sugars, eggs, and dry ingredients which have been sifted together. Add remaining ingredients. Drop by spoonfuls on cookie sheet. Bake in 350° oven about 10 minutes.

ROCKY ROAD BARS

1/4 c. sifted flour
1/4 tsp. baking powder
1/8 tsp. salt
1/3 c. packed brown sugar
1 egg

1 Tbsp. softened butter
1/2 tsp. vanilla
1/2 c. chopped walnuts or pecans
1 c. quartered marshmallows
1 (6 oz.) pkg. chocolate chips

Sift flour with baking powder and salt. Add sugar, egg, butter, and vanilla; beat smooth. Stir in 1/2 cup walnuts or pecans. Turn onto greased 9 inch square pan. Bake at 350° for 15 minutes until top is lightly browned and springs back when touched lightly. Remove from oven.

Immediately arrange marshmallows, remaining nuts, and chocolate over top. Return pan to oven immediately for 2 minutes or until chocolate is softened. Remove from oven; swirl chocolate over marshmallows and nuts. Cool until chocolate is set. Cut into bars.

TOLL HOUSE MARBLE SQUARES

1 c. plus 2 Tbsp. sifted flour
1/2 tsp. baking soda
1/2 tsp. salt
1/2 c. soft butter (or shortening)
6 Tbsp. granulated sugar
6 Tbsp. brown sugar

1/2 tsp. vanilla
1/4 tsp. water
1 egg
1/2 c. chopped nuts
6 oz. pkg. chocolate chips

Preheat oven to 375°. Sift together 1 cup plus 2 tablespoons sifted flour, soda, and salt; set aside. Blend soft butter, sugars, vanilla, and water. Beat in egg. Add flour mixture; mix well. Stir in nuts. Spread in greased 13x9x2 inch pan. Sprinkle chocolate chips over top of dough. Place in oven 2 minutes. Remove from oven and run knife through dough to marbleize. Return to oven and continue to baking at 375° for 12 to 14 minutes.

MOTHER'S DRIVING

Our mother could drive a "Model T" Ford when she was young and Clyde was a baby. Once she was sitting in the car ready to go when a friend of theirs buzzed their place in an airplane! It scared Mother and since she had the car in reverse, she hit the gas instead of the brake. Needless to say she hit a big tree. She would not drive for a long time after this!

Years layer when we were living in Channing, Butch Snyder stayed at our house a lot. He bought a new car - a 1948 Oldsmobile with hydra-matic drive. He was determined to teach Mother to drive but she always tried to turn corners at the same speed she was driving. It got to the point no one would ride with her. So ended her driving career one more time!

Jean, edited by Sue

APPLE CRUMB PIE

4 c. chopped apples
½ c. sugar
½ tsp. cinnamon
½ tsp. nutmeg
1 to 2 Tbsp. lemon juice

2 Tbsp. melted butter
2 Tbsp. sour cream
1 unbaked pie shell
Crumb Topping

Combine apples, sugar, cinnamon, nutmeg, lemon juice, butter, and sour cream; spread in pastry lined pan. Sprinkle with Crumb Topping. Bake at 425° for 15 minutes. Reduce heat to 350° and bake for 30 minutes longer or until apples are tender.

Crumb Topping:

½ c. flour
½ c. sugar

¼ c. soft butter

Combine flour and sugar; work in butter. Spread on top of apples.

ARKANSAS PIE

2 c. dried peaches
¼ c. sugar (or sugar to taste)
1 (9 inch) unbaked pie shell
2 eggs

1 tsp. vanilla
1½ c. milk
¼ c. sugar
1 Tbsp. flour

Cook dried peaches until done. Add sugar (sweeten to taste). Beat eggs well. Mix flour and sugar together. Add milk, vanilla, and beaten eggs; mix well. Place peaches in bottom of pie shell. Pour custard over peaches. Bake at 350° until custard is firm.

AUNT ANNIE PARKER'S OSGOOD PIE

1½ c. sugar
1 c. raisins, chopped
½ to 1 tsp. cinnamon
4 eggs
2 Tbsp. butter or oleo, melted

1 c. nuts, chopped
2 tsp. vanilla
¼ tsp. nutmeg
1 Tbsp. apple cider vinegar
1 (uncooked) pie shell

To plump raisins, put raisins in a small bowl and cover with hot water; cover bowl and let stand for about 10 minutes or so. Drain and chop. Beat eggs until light yellow and frothy. Add sugar and beat well. Add vanilla, cinnamon, nutmeg, vinegar, and butter; beat well. Add raisins and nuts; stir to mix. Pour into a 9 inch unbaked pie shell. Bake at 300° for about 50 minutes (or bake as you usually do a pecan pie). If pie bakes too fast, cover with foil loosely.

CHERRY PIE

1 can cherry pie filling
1 can whole cranberry sauce
1 tsp. lemon juice

1 tsp. cinnamon
¼ c. sugar

Topping:

1 c. flour
1 c. sugar

1 tsp. baking powder
1 c. milk

Mix cherry pie filling, cranberry sauce, lemon juice, cinnamon, and sugar together. Spread in bottom of baking dish. Mix flour, sugar, baking powder, and milk together; pour on top of cherry stuff. Bake at 400° for 35 minutes or until slightly browned.

CHESS PIE

3 eggs, beaten
1½ c. sugar
1 c. melted oleo
1 tsp. vanilla

2 tsp. lemon juice
3½ oz. coconut
½ c. chopped nuts

Mix eggs, sugar, oleo, vanilla, and lemon juice. Add coconut and nuts. Pour in unbaked pie shell and bake at 350° for 45 to 50 minutes.

COCONUT MERINGUE PIE

1¼ c. sugar
½ c. flour
¼ tsp. salt
3 c. milk
3 egg yolks
3 Tbsp. margarine
1 tsp. vanilla

1 c. coconut
1 baked deep pie shell
3 egg whites
¼ c. sugar
Coconut (for top)
¼ tsp. baking powder

Mix sugar, flour, and salt together. Add milk, a little at a time, until all milk is added. Cook over low heat, stirring constantly, until mixture starts to thicken. Beat egg yolks. Add small amount of cooked mixture to egg yolks. Stir well and add to pudding mixture; cook until thick. Add margarine and vanilla; cool and pour into cooled baked pie shell.

Beat egg whites until stiff. Add sugar and baking powder; beat more. Top pie with meringue. Sprinkle with coconut and bake at 375° until lightly browned.

CUSTARD PIE

4 slightly beaten eggs
1/2 c. sugar
1/4 tsp. salt
1/2 tsp. vanilla

2 1/2 c. milk, scalded
Ground nutmeg
1 (9 inch) unbaked pastry shell

Blend eggs, sugar, salt, and vanilla. Gradually stir in scalded milk. Pour into pastry shell. Sprinkle with nutmeg. Bake in 350° oven 35 to 40 minutes or till knife inserted halfway between center and edge comes out clean. Cool on rack, then chill.

Note: If desired, omit nutmeg. Sprinkle 1/2 cup flaked coconut atop unbaked filling.

FRESH PUMPKIN PIE
(Mom Willards)

1 large unbaked pie shell
2 c. fresh cooked pumpkin
1/2 can canned cream
1 c. sugar
3 eggs, beaten

1 tsp. cinnamon
1 tsp. ginger
1/2 tsp. nutmeg
1/2 tsp. salt

Peel and cook pumpkin covered in water. When tender, remove from heat. Drain well. Measure 2 cups pumpkin and mix with remaining ingredients. Bake at 300° (do not preheat oven) until set firm. Cool and top with whipped cream.

FRESH STRAWBERRY PIE

10 1/2 tsp. cornstarch
1 1/2 c. sugar
1 1/2 c. water
6 Tbsp. strawberry Jell-O

6 drops red food coloring
1 pt. fresh strawberries
1 (9 inch) baked pastry shell
1 c. Cool Whip

In saucepan, combine cornstarch, sugar, and water; mix well. Cook until thick. Remove from heat. Add Jell-O and food coloring. Stir until Jell-O is dissolved, then set aside to cool. Place fresh strawberries in cooled pie shell. Pour Jell-O mixture over strawberries. Top with Cool Whip and refrigerate. Garnish with slices of fresh strawberries if desired.

GOOD LEMON PIE

2 c. boiling water
1½ c. sugar
6½ Tbsp. cornstarch
¼ tsp. salt

1 Tbsp. grated lemon rind
3 egg yolks
¼ lb. butter
2 large or 3 medium lemons, juiced

Combine sugar, cornstarch, and salt; mix into hot water. Cook until clear and thick. Mix slightly beaten egg yolks into this mixture and cook together for about 2 minutes. Add rind, juice, and butter, then cool. Pour into a baked pie crust and cover with meringue. Brown in medium oven.

GRANDMOTHER CUNNINGHAM'S COCONUT CREAM PIE

1 c. sugar
⅓ c. flour
2 c. milk

2 egg yolks, beaten
1 tsp. vanilla extract
¾ c. coconut

Mix in order given. Cook until thick as any other cream pie. Pour into cooked pie crust, 8 or 9 inches. Beat egg whites. Add 6 soup spoons of sugar, adding a little at a time as the egg whites begin to get stiff. Beat until the meringue peaks. Add 1 teaspoon vanilla and about a cup of coconut sprinkled over the top of pie. Bake in oven until a pretty tan, approximately 10 minutes or less.

Pie Crust:

1½ c. flour
½ c. cooking oil

3 Tbsp. water

Sift flour; remove ¼ cup flour. Add water to ¼ cup flour until well mixed. Add oil to dry flour, then add the water and flour mixture to the oil and flour mixture. Mix the 2 mixtures together real well. Roll out and bake until golden brown.

HELLO DOLLY PIE

1 c. coconut
1 c. pecans
1 c. chocolate chips

1 can Eagle Brand milk
1 graham cracker crust

Combine ingredients and pour in pie crust. Bake at 350° for 30 minutes. Let cool well.

JEFF DAVIS PIE
(No relative)

3 c. sugar
1 c. butter
1 Tbsp. flour
¾ tsp. salt

1 tsp. vanilla
4 eggs, beaten
1 c. milk
2 (9 inch) unbaked pie shells

Cream sugar and butter. Blend flour, salt, and vanilla into mixture and beat well. Add eggs and then stir milk into mixture. Pour into unbaked pie shells. Bake at 450° for 10 minutes and reduce heat to 350° for 30 minutes.

JELL-O PUDDING PECAN PIE

1 (3¼ oz.) pkg. Jell-O vanilla
    pudding
1 c. corn syrup
¾ c. evaporated milk

1 egg, slightly beaten
1 c. chopped pecans
1 unbaked pie shell

Blend pudding mix with corn syrup. Gradually add milk and egg, stirring to blend. Add pecans. Pour into unbaked pie shell. Bake at 375° until top is firm and just begins to crack, about 40 minutes. Cool 3 hours. Can garnish with whipped cream and a pecan half.

LEMON MERINGUE PIE

2 egg yolks, beaten
½ c. lemon juice
1 can Eagle Brand milk
2 egg whites

¼ tsp. baking powder
3 Tbsp. sugar
1 baked pie shell

Mix together egg yolks, lemon juice, and Eagle Brand milk. Pour into baked pie shell. Beat egg whites until stiff. Add sugar gradually and then baking powder. Top pie filling with meringue and bake in slow oven until top is brown.

1615-94

87

MAMAW PIPPIN'S CHOCOLATE PIE

1 baked pie crust
¾ c. sugar
¼ c. cocoa
2 Tbsp. flour

1½ c. milk
2 egg yolks
⅛ tsp. salt
1 tsp. vanilla

Mix sugar, cocoa, and flour in saucepan. Add milk and stir until hot. Beat egg yolks in separate bowl and add to this ½ cup of hot mixture. Mix well and return to pan. Cook until thick and add salt and vanilla. Pour into crust. Top with meringue while hot.

Meringue:

3 egg whites
6 Tbsp. sugar

½ tsp. cream of tartar

Let egg whites come to room temperature (about 30 minutes). Whip egg whites and cream of tartar to soft peak stage. Add sugar slowly, 1 tablespoon at a time. Beat until stiff peaks form. Spread meringue over hot pie filling. Seal meringue to crust so meringue doesn't shrink. Bake in a 350° oven for 12 to 15 minutes or until golden brown.

MOTHER'S CARAMEL PIE

2 c. white sugar
3 c. milk
2 beaten egg yolks

2 Tbsp. flour
2 Tbsp. butter

Topping:

2 egg whites
2 Tbsp. sugar

¼ tsp. baking powder

Put white sugar in cast iron skillet. Melt, stirring constantly, until sugar is brown. Add milk and boil until all sugar is dissolved. Add beaten egg yolks. Add flour, dissolved in small amount of water (no lumps). Add butter and cook until thick. Pour into baked pie shell. Beat egg whites. Add sugar and baking powder. Put on top of pie and brown in slow oven.

MYSTERY PIE

3 egg whites
1 c. sugar
1 tsp. vanilla
¼ tsp. salt

¼ tsp. cream of tartar
22 Ritz crackers, crumbled
1 c. chopped pecans

Beat egg whites. Add sugar. Mix in other ingredients. Put in a greased 9x9 inch pan and bake at 350° for 30 to 40 minutes.

PECAN CREAM PIE

1 c. sugar
3 heaping Tbsp. flour
¼ tsp. salt
1½ c. milk

1 Tbsp. butter
3 egg yolks, beaten
½ c. chopped pecans
1 baked pie shell

Stir all together and cook until thick, stirring constantly. Add 1 teaspoon vanilla and pour into baked pie shell.

Meringue Topping:

3 egg whites
6 Tbsp. sugar

¼ tsp. baking powder

Beat egg whites. Add baking powder and sugar, 1 tablespoon at a time, after it starts looking foamy. Beat until stiff peaks form. Spread meringue on pie filling. Seal meringue to crust and bake at 350° for 12 to 15 minutes or until golden brown.

PECAN PIE

1½ c. brown sugar
½ c. white sugar
2 Tbsp. flour
1 tsp. salt
½ c. canned milk

2 eggs (1 at a time)
½ c. water
1 tsp. vanilla
2 Tbsp. margarine
1½ c. pecans

Mix dry ingredients together. Add canned milk, beaten eggs (1 at a time), water, vanilla, and soft margarine. Put pecans into unbaked pie shell. Pour mixture over pecans and bake at 350°.

PINEAPPLE CREAM CUSTARD PIE

4 large eggs, separated
2 tsp. vanilla
2¼ c. sugar
2 heaping Tbsp. flour

1 c. thick cream
1 large can crushed pineapple
1 tsp. salt
2 (9 inch) unbaked pie shells

Separate eggs. Beat egg whites stiff and add ¼ cup sugar and 1 teaspoon vanilla; set aside. Beat egg yolks until lemon colored. Add salt and continue beating. Add cream and beat as if whipping cream. Add 1½ cups sugar gradually. Beat until thickens slightly, then add remaining ½ cup sugar with flour stirred into sugar very well. When mixture looks like cake dough, add pineapple and 1 teaspoon vanilla; mix well. Fold in egg whites. Dip into unbaked pie shells. Bake at 450° for 10 minutes, then at 350° for 30 minutes. Check for doneness. If more cooking is needed, reduce oven to 300° for 5 to 15 minutes.

REALLY RICH PECAN PIE

1½ c. Mrs. Butterworth's syrup
¼ c. margarine
¼ c. sugar
1½ c. chopped pecans

3 eggs, slightly beaten
1½ tsp. vanilla
Dash of salt
1 unbaked pie shell

Heat oven to 375°. Combine syrup, margarine, and sugar in saucepan. Bring to a boil; boil gently for 5 minutes, uncovered, stirring occasionally. Cool slightly. Put pecans in pie shell. Mix eggs, vanilla, and salt in a bowl. Gradually stir in cooled syrup mixture. Pour over pecans in pie shell. Bake 35 to 40 minutes or until knife comes out clean. Cool on wire rack.

RED CHERRY PIE

1 c. sugar
4 Tbsp. flour
¼ tsp. almond extract
½ tsp. cinnamon

2½ c. sour red cherries and juice
(No. 2 can)
2 Tbsp. butter

Combine first 4 ingredients in saucepan; stir in cherries and juice. Cook over moderate heat, stirring constantly, until mixture thickens and boils. Pour into pie shell (9 inch); dot with butter. Cover with top crust. Bake in 425° oven for 30 to 40 minutes or until browned and juice bubbles through slits in crust.

SOUTHERN CHESS PIE
(Pecan)

1 c. brown sugar, packed
½ c. granulated sugar
1 Tbsp. flour
2 eggs

2 Tbsp. milk
1 tsp. vanilla
½ c. butter, melted
1 c. pecans or walnuts

Originally from England, a delicacy of nuts and transparent custard.

Make pastry for 8 inch, 1 crust pie. Mix brown sugar, granulated sugar, and flour; beat in thoroughly the eggs, milk, vanilla, and butter. Fold in pecans or walnuts. Pour into pastry-lined pie pan. Bake 40 to 50 minutes at 375° just until set. Serve slightly warm, plain or with whipped cream.

SHOO-FLY PIE

1 unbaked pastry shell
½ c. dark molasses
½ c. boiling water

½ tsp. baking soda
1 large egg

Crumb Mixture:

¼ c. shortening
2 c. flour
½ c. brown sugar

Dash of salt
¼ tsp. cinnamon

Prepare 1 unbaked pastry shell. Mix together molasses, boiling water, soda, and egg. Pour into pie shell. Top with Crumb Mixture made by cutting shortening into mixture of flour, brown sugar, salt, and cinnamon. Bake 1 to 1¼ hours at 350°.

VINEGAR PIE

9 inch baked pie shell
3 egg yolks, beaten
1 c. sugar
¼ tsp. salt
1¾ c. boiling water

¼ c. cider vinegar
¼ c. cornstarch
¼ c. cold water
1 tsp. lemon extract
Meringue (3 egg whites)

Place egg yolks in top of double boiler. Add sugar and salt. Gradually add boiling water, stirring constantly. Add vinegar and cornstarch, dissolved in cold water. Cook over boiling water until thick and smooth, about 12 minutes. Remove from heat. Add lemon extract. Stir until filling is smooth and blended, scraping sides of pan. Pour hot filling into pie shell. Top lukewarm filling with meringue, spreading to edges and sealing to crust. Bake in 350° oven 12 to 15 minutes or until meringue is lightly browned.

MOTHER'S APPLE PEELING FRIED PIES

Apple peelings
Cinnamon

Sugar
Butter

Our mother never wasted anything. When canning apples, she would cook the peelings until tender, then drain. Add sugar, cinnamon, and butter to taste. Make into fried pies using the Fried Pie Crust recipe.

MOTHER'S CHOCOLATE FRIED PIES

1 c. sugar
2 or 3 Tbsp. cocoa

⅓ c. oleo, melted
Crust (from fried pies)

Mix sugar, cocoa, and oleo together. Mixture should be thick. Use crust for fried pies. Cook in hot shortening or oil. Cook on each side until golden brown. Drain on brown paper.

Chocolate Pies can also be baked in 400° oven for 9 to 10 minutes. Make sure to seal the edges well or they will break open.

1615-94

APRICOT FRIED PIES

1 lb. dried apricots
1½ c. sugar
Dash of salt

½ tsp. nutmeg
¼ c. butter
1 tsp. lemon juice

Soak apricots overnight. Cover apricots with water and bring to a boil; reduce heat and simmer, uncovered, 30 minutes. Drain some juice if needed. Add sugar, salt, nutmeg, butter, and lemon juice. Find "Pie Crust for Fried Pies" in this book and follow directions. Put 1 to 2 tablespoons of fruit on pie crust and fry in hot shortening.

Note: Might need to mash apricots after cooking if still pretty lumpy.

Pie Crust for Fried Pies:

3 c. flour
1 c. butter flavor shortening
1 tsp. salt

1 egg, slightly beaten (then water to make ¾ c.)

Mix flour, shortening, and salt, a little at a time. Mix in egg-water mixture. Make into a ball and wrap in Saran Wrap. Chill.

For Fried Pies, roll into dollar size balls, then roll between waxed paper the size of a 3 pound shortening can lid. Put 1 to 2 tablespoons of fruit mixture on 1 side, leaving 1 inch space on the outside to seal. Moisten around outside; fold over and press edges with fingers. Crimp with a fork dipped in flour to seal. Cook in hot shortening about 375°. Cook on each side until golden brown. Drain on paper towels and cover with paper towels and cloth to keep from collecting moisture.

FRIED PIES

Dried apples, peaches, or apricots
Sugar

Corn starch

Dried fruit makes the best filling. Soak dried fruit, apples, peaches, and apricots in warm water. (Don't use too much water.) Cook in saucepan (stirring constantly or it will stick) until fruit is done. Add sugar and corn starch, mixed together. Sugar amount depends on fruit. Apricots need more sugar usually. Canned fruit can be used; needs to be cooked down with sugar and corn starch or flour. Set fruit aside.

Fried Pie Dough:

5 c. flour
1 Tbsp. sugar
12 oz. can milk

1 c. Crisco
2 tsp. salt
1 egg

Mix and roll out fairly thin. Cut the size of a saucer. Fill with fruit; moisten inside edge with water. Mash together with tines of fork. Fry in deep fat; drain on paper towels *or* brown paper.

APPLE CRISP COBBLER

16 oz. pkg. dried apples
1 c. orange juice
1 c. sugar
1 tsp. cinnamon

1½ c. flour
1 c. sugar
1 tsp. salt
¾ c. oleo

Soak 16 ounce package dried apples overnight. To cook, bring to a boil, then simmer for 30 minutes; drain. Arrange apples in greased 14 inch Dutch oven. Pour 1 cup orange juice over apples. Combine 1 cup sugar and 1 teaspoon cinnamon. Sprinkle over apples. Combine flour, sugar, and salt. Cut in oleo into dry ingredients until crumbly. Spoon mixture over apples and bake until done (about 30 minutes).

APPLE CRUMB COBBLER

8 c. apples, peeled and sliced
1 c. sugar
1 tsp. cinnamon
1 tsp. nutmeg

3 or 4 Tbsp. lemon juice
4 Tbsp. sour cream
4 Tbsp. melted oleo

Combine all ingredients and pour into a greased 14 inch Dutch oven. Sprinkle with Crumb Topping. Cook with slow coals under oven and hot coals on lid until crust is done and apples are tender. Bake 45 to 60 minutes in regular oven at 350°.

Crumb Topping:

1½ c. flour
1 c. sugar

1 c. soft oleo
Dash of salt

Combine flour, sugar, and salt; work in oleo.

COWBOY'S PUDDIN' PIE

1 c. flour
½ c. sugar
2 eggs
2 Tbsp. oleo

1½ c. milk
1 tsp. vanilla
1 Tbsp. baking powder
½ tsp. salt

Beat eggs and milk until well mixed. Add salt, baking powder, sugar, and vanilla. Mix thoroughly, then add flour and stir until it forms a smooth batter. Add melted oleo and mix. Place this batter in a greased Dutch oven.

In a small pan, heat 1 can presweetened fruit of your choice or if water packed fruit is used add 1 to 1½ cups sugar to the fruit and heat until sugar is melted. Pour fruit over batter and bake until batter rises to the top and becomes a golden brown.

DADDY'S CHERRY COBBLER

8 cans tart canned cherries
Sugar to taste

1 white cake mix

Mix all ingredients and let boil down till juice is thick. Roll out biscuit dough real thin and put on top. Bake till crust is done. Butter crust when done.

DADDY'S COBBLER (QUICK)
(Dutch oven)

2 cans fruit, sweetened to taste (any
   canned fruit - fruit cocktail,
   peaches, or cherries, etc.)

1 box cake mix
¼ lb. butter

Melt butter in bottom of Dutch oven. Sprinkle in cake mix. Pour sweetened fruit on top. Bake with low coals on bottom and top of Dutch oven.

DRIED PEACH COBBLER

1 (8 oz.) pkg. dried peaches
1½ c. sugar
1 tsp. almond extract

3 Tbsp. butter
½ tsp. salt

Soak peaches 2 hours or until soft. Simmer until done. Add butter, sugar, and salt. Stir well and put back on heat until sugar is dissolved (very low heat so peaches don't stick). Remove from heat and add almond extract. Pour into Dutch oven, sprayed with nonstick spray. This makes Dutch oven easier to clean.

Top with sourdough starter crust or your favorite crust. Bake with a few coals under oven and a few on top until crust is golden brown.

DRIED PEACH COBBLER SOURDOUGH CRUST

1¼ c. Crisco
3 c. flour
1 tsp. salt
2 Tbsp. sugar

¾ c. sourdough starter
1 tsp. cinnamon
½ tsp. baking powder

Cut Crisco into flour until crumbly. Add other dry ingredients; mix well. Add starter and make ball. Roll out thinly ¼ to ⅜ inch thick. Cut with small biscuit cutter (I use Campbell's soup can). Place biscuits on top of cobbler and bake in Dutch oven.

DRIED PEACH COBBLER WITH SOURDOUGH CRUST

3 c. sugar
Dash of salt
½ c. butter
2 tsp. lemon juice

2 tsp. almond extract
2 tsp. cinnamon
1½ lb. dried peaches

Soak peaches overnight. Bring to a boil. Reduce heat and simmer, uncovered, for 30 minutes. Add more water if needed. Add sugar, salt, butter, lemon juice, extract, and cinnamon. Thicken if needed; set aside.

Sourdough Crust:

2 c. sugar
2 c. flour
4 tsp. baking powder
¼ tsp. salt
½ c. butter

1 c. milk
1 c. sourdough starter
2 tsp. vanilla
½ tsp. cinnamon

Melt butter in 14 inch Dutch oven. Mix crust ingredients and pour into butter. Pour peach mixture in last. Bake 25 to 30 minutes on slow coals with hot coals on top of lid. Make sure batter is done.

FLOATING CHERRY COBBLER

2 c. flour
4 Tbsp. butter, melted
1½ c. milk
2 c. sugar

4 tsp. baking powder
2 c. pitted cherries
2 c. sugar

Mix flour, butter, milk, sugar, and baking powder; pour in the bottom of a 12 inch Dutch oven. Drain cherries and reserve juice. Pour cherries over batter, then add 2 cups sugar. Add enough water to juice to make 2 cups. Pour over all and bake with slow coals under oven and hot coals on lid until crust is done, 350° in regular oven.

1615-94

PEACH COBBLER

1 gal. peaches, sliced (less 2 c. juice)
2½ c. sugar
⅓ c. oleo

2 tsp. almond extract
¼ tsp. cinnamon
Dash of salt
8 Tbsp. corn starch

Mix all ingredients and thicken peaches with corn starch and water over fire. Can use flour and water. Cover with crust. Punch holes to let out steam and cook with slow coals under oven and hot coals on lid until crust is done. Or, cook 30 minutes or so in 400° oven.

Crust:

1 c. butter flavor Crisco
3 c. flour

1 tsp. salt
1 egg and water to make ¾ c.

Cut Crisco into flour and salt. Add egg mixture. Roll out and cover the fruit. Use ¾ of recipe for 14 inch Dutch oven.

QUICK APPLE COBBLER

½ c. oleo
2 c. sugar
2 c. flour
½ tsp. cinnamon
4 tsp. baking powder

⅛ tsp. salt
2 c. milk
2 tsp. vanilla extract
1 gal. sweetened apples

Melt oleo in 14 inch Dutch oven. Mix batter: Sugar, flour, cinnamon, baking powder, salt, milk, and vanilla extract. Pour into oleo, then put apples in last. Bake 25 to 30 minutes on slow coals with hot coals on top of lid. Be sure batter is done. If not cooking on coals, cook in oven at 375°.

QUICK PEACH COBBLER

¾ c. oleo
3¾ c. sugar
3 c. flour
½ tsp. cinnamon
6 tsp. baking powder

3 dashes of salt
3 c. milk
3 tsp. almond extract
1½ gal. sliced peaches (don't use all the juice)

Melt oleo in 16 inch Dutch oven. Mix batter: Sugar, flour, cinnamon, baking powder, salt, milk, and extract. Pour into oleo, then put peaches in last. Bake 25 to 30 minutes with slow coals under oven and hot coals on lid until done. Be sure batter is done. If not cooking on coals, cook in oven at 375°.

APPLE CRISP

6 apples, peeled and sliced
¼ c. brown sugar
¼ c. melted oleo
⅔ c. flour
⅓ c. brown sugar (more)

⅛ tsp. salt
¼ tsp. soda
1 tsp. cinnamon
⅔ c. oatmeal
½ c. chopped pecans

1. Peel and slice apples. Sprinkle ¼ cup brown sugar over apples. Dot with oleo.

2. Mix oleo, flour, brown sugar, salt, soda, cinnamon, oatmeal, and pecans together; sprinkle over apples. Bake in a 9x13 inch pan for 40 minutes at 350°.

BANANA PUDDING

6 bananas, sliced
1 large instant vanilla pudding mix
   (use 3 c. milk instead of 4)

1 large Cool Whip
1 (7½ oz.) jar marshmallow cream
1 box vanilla wafers

Mix pudding mix as directed. Add Cool Whip, then add marshmallow cream, bananas, and vanilla wafers. *Very good.*

BREAD PUDDING

4 eggs
1½ c. sugar
1 tsp. vanilla
½ tsp. cinnamon (optional)
5 large biscuits (or 5 slices light
   bread)

1 (12 oz.) can evaporated milk
½ can water
¾ c. raisins
½ tsp. nutmeg
2 to 3 Tbsp. margarine

Mix eggs, sugar, vanilla, and cinnamon; beat well. Tear bread into small pieces. Add to other mixture. Add milk and water to other mixture and beat well. Add raisins if desired. Let mixture set 5 to 10 minutes to let bread soften. (If it seems too dry, add a little water.) Pour into a buttered 10x10x2 inch pan. Sprinkle about ½ teaspoon nutmeg over top if desired. Dot with margarine. Bake at 350° for 30 to 45 minutes. *Do not* overcook - will be jiggly in center like a custard pie. *Good warm.*

Make a plain vanilla sauce to serve (warm) over cold pudding if you like. You may add chopped nuts or coconut in pudding if you desire.

SPOTTED PUP (RICE PUDDING)

2 c. leftover cooked rice
1 c. sugar
1 tsp. cinnamon
1 tsp. nutmeg

1 tsp. vanilla
2 c. milk
3 eggs
1 c. raisins

Heat milk to boiling. Slightly beat eggs, sugar, and vanilla. Stir until smooth. Add remaining ingredients. Pour into Dutch oven and bake in slow oven until egg mixture is done and raisins soft. Can be baked at 375° for 25 minutes or until knife inserted comes out clean.

CHERRY TORTE

1 c. cake flour
5 Tbsp. powdered sugar
½ c. oleo
2 eggs
1½ c. sugar

¼ tsp. salt
¼ c. flour
¾ c. chopped pecans
1 tsp. vanilla
1 can sour cherries, drained

Blend 1 cup flour, powdered sugar, and oleo; press into bottom of large baking dish. Bake at 350° for 15 minutes. Beat eggs. Add dry ingredients, vanilla, nuts, and cherries. Pour over baked crust and bake 30 minutes at 350°. Serve with ice cream or whipped cream.

CHOCOLATE GRAVY

2 c. milk
½ c. butter
4 Tbsp. flour
3 Tbsp. cocoa

1¼ c. sugar
Dash of salt
Drop or 2 of vanilla

Mix dry ingredients, then add vanilla, butter, and milk. Cook over low heat until pretty thick. Can be used for fried pies. Use pie crust or canned biscuits.

CHOCOLATE PUDDING DESSERT

Crust:

1 c. flour   ½ c. oleo
1 c. chopped nuts

Mix and press into 9x13 inch dish. Bake at 350° for 20 minutes.

Cheese:

1 (8 oz.) pkg. cream cheese   1 c. Cool Whip
1 c. powdered sugar

Mix and spread on cooled crust.

Pudding:

1 small pkg. instant chocolate   3 c. milk (only)
    pudding mix
1 small pkg. instant vanilla pudding
    mix

Mix puddings together and spread on cheese mixture. Top with remainder of large carton of Cool Whip and chopped nuts.

DUTCH OVEN BREAD PUDDING

About 20 old biscuits   ½ c. melted butter
4 Tbsp. cinnamon   1 c. sugar
4 eggs   4 c. scalded milk (or can use 2 c.
1 tsp. salt   evaporated milk with 2 c. water)

Scald milk and set aside. Beat eggs. Add sugar, butter, salt, and eggs to milk; mix well. Spray Dutch oven with nonstick spray. Tear up biscuits in oven. Sprinkle cinnamon on bread. Add milk mixture and bake in Dutch oven with coals on top and coals on bottom. Pour the following sauce recipe on top and serve. May put nuts or raisins in bread pudding.

DUTCH OVEN BREAD PUDDING SAUCE

2 c. sugar   1 tsp. salt
½ c. flour   2 c. milk, scalded (can use ½
2 eggs, beaten   evaporated and ½ water)
2 tsp. vanilla   3 Tbsp. butter

Combine sugar, flour, and salt together. Gradually add milk, keeping smooth. Heat over low heat until it starts to thicken. Add small amount of sauce to beaten eggs and stir well, then add eggs to cooking mixture. Cook until desired thickness (consistency of 40 weight oil). Remove from heat; cool and add butter and vanilla. Pour over Dutch Oven Bread Pudding.

VINEGAR PUDDING

¼ c. apple vinegar
2 c. water
1 c. sugar
1 tsp. vanilla

1¼ c. flour
½ tsp. salt
½ c. shortening
4 Tbsp. water

Mix flour, salt, and shortening, cutting in shortening until well mixed with flour and salt. Add the 4 tablespoons water and mix until dough holds together. Divide into 3 equal parts. Roll each into a sheet about ¼ inch thick. Cut into strips about 1 inch wide. Mix all the other ingredients in small Dutch oven and bring to boil.

While mixture is boiling, cut the strips of pastry into short lengths and drop into boiling liquid until 2 parts of pastry are used. Remove oven from heat and use the third part of the pastry to crisscross the pudding with the long strips. Sprinkle with 2 tablespoons margarine cut in small pieces and bake until top is brown.

HOMEMADE ICE CREAM

4 eggs, beaten
1½ c. sugar
1 pt. whipping cream
1 pt. half & half

1 can Eagle Brand milk
2 Tbsp. vanilla
Milk (to fill freezer)

Beat eggs. Add sugar, Eagle Brand milk, whipping cream, half & half, and vanilla; mix well. Pour into freezer and fill to top with milk. May add fruit and/or nuts of your choice before adding milk to fill line. Freeze according to freezer directions.

KEN'S BANANA NUT ICE CREAM

3 eggs, beaten
2 c. sugar
1 Tbsp. vanilla
3 bananas, mashed

1 can Eagle Brand milk
1 c. chopped pecans
1 pt. half & half

Blend all the above and add sweet milk to make 1 gallon; freeze.

GRANN PHOEBE'S REFRIGERATOR ICE CREAM

2 tsp. flour or corn starch
2 Tbsp. cold milk
1 c. cream
¾ to 1 c. sugar

2 tsp. vanilla
Dash of salt
3 c. whipping cream, whipped

Dissolve flour or corn starch and cold milk. Heat, but do not boil, the cream. Add sugar until dissolved. Add vanilla and salt. Cool and mix well with flour-milk mixture. Pour into ice trays and chill. Beat thoroughly and add whipped cream. Freeze all mixture, stirring occasionally.

Note: To freeze cream in refrigerator trays, it is advisable to add some thickening to the substance. Cream must be whipped and folded into other ingredients just before mixture is put in refrigerator trays.

SNOW ICE CREAM

2 eggs
1 can evaporated milk (or other milk)

1 c. sugar
2 tsp. vanilla
Dash of salt

Beat eggs very well. Add remaining ingredients and blend together until well mixed. Fill a bowl with snow. Pour mixture over it until you get the right consistency.

Notes

Miscellaneous

TEMPERATURE TESTS
FOR CANDY MAKING

There are two different methods of determining when candy has been cooked to the proper consistency. One is by using a candy thermometer in order to record degrees, the other is by using the cold water test. The chart below will prove useful in helping to follow candy recipes:

TYPE OF CANDY	DEGREES	COLD WATER
Fondant, Fudge	234 - 238°	Soft Ball
Divinity, Caramels	245 - 248°	Firm Ball
Taffy	265 - 270°	Hard Ball
Butterscotch	275 - 280°	Light Crack
Peanut Brittle	285 - 290°	Hard Crack
Caramelized Sugar	310 - 321°	Caramelized

In using the cold water test, use a fresh cupful of cold water for each test. When testing, remove the candy from the fire and pour about ½ teaspoon of candy into the cold water. Pick the candy up in the fingers and roll into a ball if possible.

In the SOFT BALL TEST the candy will roll into a soft ball which quickly loses its shape when removed from the water.

In the FIRM BALL TEST the candy will roll into a firm, but not hard ball. It will flatten out a few minutes after being removed from the water.

In the HARD BALL TEST the candy will roll into a hard ball which has lost almost all plasticity and will roll around on a plate on removal from the water.

In the LIGHT CRACK TEST the candy will form brittle threads which will soften on removal from the water.

In the HARD CRACK TEST the candy will form brittle threads in the water which will remain brittle after being removed from the water.

In CARAMELIZING the sugar first melts then becomes a golden brown. It will form a hard brittle ball in cold water.

MISCELLANEOUS

MOTHER AND DADDY

Our mother was always a very strong believer of the Church of Christ. She and some other people in Channing decided to start a church. They first held services in the court house, then they fixed up an old house and later built a church.

Daddy grew up a Methodist. Several years before he passed away, he felt the need to make peace with the Lord. He contacted Tommy Mullins and made arrangements to be baptized in Sidle Springs - running spring water. He felt it would take plenty of running water to wash his sins away.

Jean, edited by Sue

CHRISTMAS WREATHS

½ c. oleo
3 c. large marshmallows

½ tsp. green cake coloring
4½ c. corn flakes

Melt oleo, marshmallows, and cake coloring together. Add corn flakes. Shape in wreaths. Decorate with red hots.

Dampen fingers in cold water to make them easier to shape.

DIVINITY CANDY

2 c. sugar
¼ tsp. cream of tartar

½ c. Karo
½ c. water

Boil to *hard ball* stage and beat into 2 egg whites, beaten to stiff peaks. Add nuts and teaspoon vanilla when candy begins to hold shape. Stir until it begins to harden and drop from spoon onto waxed paper.

EASY PRALINES

1 pkg. butterscotch pudding mix
   (not "instant" kind)
1 c. sugar
½ c. brown sugar

½ c. evaporated milk
1 Tbsp. butter
1½ c. pecan halves

1. Mix butterscotch pudding mix, sugar, brown sugar, milk, and butter in a heavy 1½ quart saucepan.
2. Cook and stir to a full, all-over boil, then boil slowly 3 to 5 minutes until mixture reaches soft ball stage. Take off heat.
3. Stir in pecans. Beat until mixture begins to thicken, but still looks shiny.
4. Drop tablespoonfuls of mixture quickly onto waxed paper to form 3 inch pralines. If mixture thickens and starts to lose its shine, add a few drops of milk before dropping more pralines. Let pralines stand until firm. Makes about 18.

MEXICAN FUDGE

5 c. sugar (total)
1 large can milk
1 c. oleo
1 c. Eagle Brand milk

1 pt. marshmallow whip
2 tsp. vanilla
4 c. pecans

Mix 4 cups sugar, can of milk, oleo, and Eagle Brand milk together; bring to a boil over low medium heat. While cooking, pour 1 cup sugar in a heavy skillet; brown and when it's bubbling all over, cook ½ minute. Do not burn. Pour browned sugar syrup into first mixture and cook to soft ball stage. Remove from heat and add 1 pint marshmallow whip. Beat 5 minutes on high with mixer, then place in cold water. Beat for 5 more minutes. Add vanilla and pecans; beat until dull. Pour on greased platter or pans. Makes a lot.

MICROWAVE BRITTLE

1 c. raw peanuts or pecans halves
or almonds
1 c. sugar
½ c. white syrup

⅛ tsp. salt
1 Tbsp. butter
1 tsp. baking soda
1 tsp. vanilla

Stir together your choice of nuts, sugar, syrup, and salt in 1½ quart casserole. Place in microwave oven and cook 7 to 8 minutes, stirring well after 4 minutes. Add butter and blend well. Return to oven and cook 2 to 3 minutes more or until nuts are golden brown. Add baking soda and vanilla; gently stir until light and foamy. Pour onto greased cooking sheet and let cool. When cool, break into pieces and store in airtight container.

PECAN BRITTLE

2 c. sugar
½ c. light corn syrup
1 c. butter
½ tsp. salt

1 tsp. baking soda
1 tsp. vanilla
5 c. broken pecans

Toast pecans in 200° oven until warm. In a large saucepan, combine sugar, corn syrup, and butter; cook on high heat, stirring constantly, until it reaches 290° on a candy thermometer. Remove from heat; stir in salt, soda, vanilla, and nuts. Beat quickly. Spread on greased marble slab or heavily greased cookie sheet. Break into pieces when cool.

NEVER FAIL FUDGE

1 (13 oz.) can evaporated milk
¼ lb. butter
4 c. sugar

12 oz. pkg. chocolate chips
7 oz. jar marshmallow cream
1 c. chopped nuts

Place contents of milk, butter, and sugar in saucepan. Bring to boil, stirring constantly, to medium soft ball stage when tested in cold water. Remove from heat and fold in chocolate chips and marshmallow cream. Stir until blended. Add chopped nuts if desired. Pour in greased pan. Cool and place in refrigerator until ready to slice in squares.

PEANUT BUTTER BONBONS

2 c. peanut butter
4½ c. powdered sugar
½ c. butter

3 c. Rice Krispies
2 (12 oz.) pkg. chocolate chips

Melt peanut butter and butter. Add cereal and sugar. Form into balls and chill. Melt chocolate chips and dip balls in it. Add some paraffin to chips when melting. Add butter to balls, if needed, when shaping into balls. Makes 100.

PEANUT PATTIES

3 c. sugar
1 c. Karo

1 c. water
1 lb. (raw) peanuts

Mix sugar, Karo, and water; bring to a rolling boil. Add red color and peanuts. Cook till hard boil stage. Add ½ stick butter and ½ teaspoon salt. Beat until thicker. Spoon out onto waxed paper very quickly as it sets up fast.

MARSH-MALO FUDGE

2¼ c. sugar
¼ c. butter
¾ c. evaporated milk
1 c. chopped pecans

5 oz. marshmallow cream
1½ pkg. Hershey's semi-sweet
    chocolate chips

Mix sugar, butter, milk, and marshmallow cream; bring to boil and boil for 4 minutes, stirring constantly. Remove from heat. Add chocolate chips; stir until chips are dissolved. Pour into buttered dish. Cool. Makes 2¼ pounds fudge.

TEXAS MILLIONAIRES

1 c. brown sugar
1 c. white sugar
1 c. red Karo

1 c. oleo
2 c. canned milk
1 tsp. vanilla

Mix all ingredients *except* 1 cup milk; stir well. Let come to a boil, stirring constantly. Add other cup of milk slowly (do not stop boil). Cook until it forms a soft ball (this takes a long time). Add 1 pound pecan halves. Pour into a large buttered cookie sheet and let stand in icebox overnight. Cut in squares. Dip in chocolate.

Dip:

12 oz. sweet or semi-sweet
    chocolate or chocolate chips

1 (¼ lb.) bar paraffin

Melt together over hot water. After dipping, set on wax paper.

BARBECUE SAUCE

1 medium chopped onion
2 Tbsp. butter
2 Tbsp. vinegar
2 Tbsp. brown sugar
4 Tbsp. lemon juice
1 c. catsup

½ c. water
½ Tbsp. prepared mustard
3 Tbsp. Worcestershire sauce
¼ tsp. salt
¼ tsp. cayenne pepper
¼ tsp. crushed red pepper

Brown onion in butter. Add remaining ingredients; simmer 30 minutes, then pour over beef, pork ribs, or goat.

GOING TO THE WAGON

When we were growing up in Channing, Texas, at one time our dad and all 3 of our brothers were working at the Matador Ranch. They would get a day off or a week-end off now and then and would all come to town. The Shepherd house was always a home away from home for the cowboys. Our mother would always have to go upstairs and count heads to know how many to cook breakfast for. She was a second mother to the cowboys, and since we lived in an 11 room house we had plenty of room.

We girls would go to the Matador Ranch Wagon every chance we got. We loved eating at the chuckwagon and learned something about cooking on a chuckwagon way back then.

We always went to the wagon to agitate the cowboys and help the cook, especially clean up. In fact, that is where I met my husband, Wayne Cates, the first time. We were 13 or 14 years of age. Wayne's Great Uncle Sam Cates was the wagon cook at the Matadors at that time. I met Wayne a few years later when I was filling in as cook at the J A Ranch, when Clyde's wife, Beverly, had their first daughter, Linda.

Jean, edited by Sue

"Ten Minutes to Coffee"

Moving roundup camp with the chuck wagon leading and the remunda trailing along, the wagon boss visits with the cook while he waits for the outfit to reach the new camp grounds where they'll enjoy a cup of that vital brew.

CHEESE SAUCE

¼ c. butter
¼ c. flour
5 c. milk
Salt to taste

Pepper to taste
¼ tsp. nutmeg
¼ c. half & half (if desired)
½ c. Parmesan cheese

Melt butter in large skillet. Add flour and allow it to bubble 1 to 2 minutes, stirring with a whisk. Add milk and stir. Cook slowly, about 20 to 30 minutes. Add salt, pepper, and nutmeg to flavor. For a richer sauce, add half & half. Stir in cheese. Serve over noodles, macaroni, or spaghetti.

CHOCOLATE SAUCE

1 c. chocolate chips
¾ c. water
¾ c. light corn syrup
½ c. sugar

¼ tsp. salt
1 Tbsp. butter
1 tsp. vanilla

In a 1 quart saucepan over low heat, melt chocolate in water, stirring until mixture is thick and smooth. Gradually stir in syrup, sugar, salt, and butter. Stirring constantly, bring to a boil. Off heat, stir in vanilla; cool. Makes 2 cups.

HOT SAUCE

3 qt. tomatoes, chopped
12 jalapeno peppers, chopped
4 large onions, chopped

Garlic to taste
Salt to taste
½ c. vinegar

Bring to a boil, then simmer for about 1 hour or until vegetables are done. Pour into hot jars and seal.

SPAGHETTI SAUCE

¼ c. oil
1 clove garlic
1 medium onion, chopped
½ green pepper, chopped
1 (6 oz.) can tomato paste
Salt and pepper

1 (16 oz.) can tomato sauce
1 (16 oz.) can tomatoes
½ tsp. oregano
½ tsp. basil
1 bay leaf
2 c. water

Mix all ingredients and simmer an hour or 2; spoon over spaghetti.

WHITE SAUCE

2 Tbsp. oleo
2 Tbsp. flour

1 c. milk

Melt oleo. Add flour and stir quickly over low heat until smooth. Add milk and stir until thickened.

Variation: Add ½ cup grated cheese. Add 1 tablespoon minced parsley. Add ½ cup chopped mushrooms.

BREAKFAST BURRITOS (BULLETS)

1 lb. sausage
1 doz. eggs
1 onion, chopped
8 oz. grated cheese

1 (4 oz.) can chopped green chilies
Picante sauce
1 pkg. flour tortillas

In a Dutch oven, crumble and brown sausage; drain. Add eggs and scramble with sausage. Heat flour tortillas on Dutch oven lid over fire. Top flour tortillas with sausage-egg mixture, then add onions, green chilies, cheese, and picante sauce. Roll up and eat.

MOTHER'S WHOLE WHEAT BREAKFAST

Use 2 cups whole wheat (not treated), wash thoroughly. Make sure wheat has not been treated for planting.

Our mother used to soak whole wheat grains. Cover in water and allow room for swelling. Soak overnight. The next morning, cook until tender. Serve while hot with cream or milk, sugar and butter.

RANCHER OMELET

6 slices bacon, diced
2 Tbsp. finely chopped onion
1 c. grated potato
6 large eggs, slightly beaten

½ tsp. salt
Pepper to taste
2 Tbsp. minced parsley (optional)
Dash of Tabasco

Fry bacon until crisp; remove from pan and drain. Leave at least 2 tablespoons of bacon grease. Add onion and saute over low heat until soft. Add grated potatoes and cook until light brown. Mix together eggs, salt, pepper, and Tabasco; pour into pan. As omelet cooks, lift up edges with spatula to let egg mixture slide under. When firm, sprinkle omelet with crumbled crisp bacon and parsley. Fold over and serve. Serves 6.

CHOW-CHOW

1 gal. chopped cabbage
1 doz. chopped onions
½ doz. green (bell) peppers
½ gal. chopped green tomatoes
½ doz. red (bell) peppers
½ c. salt (not iodized)

1 gal. vinegar
2 lb. sugar
½ c. ground mustard
6 Tbsp. white mustard seed
3 Tbsp. celery seed
1 Tbsp. cloves

Put cabbage, onions, green peppers, green tomatoes, red peppers, and sprinkle of salt in mesh bag; let hang and drip overnight. Next morning, put vinegar, sugar, mustard, mustard seed, and celery in pot. Put cloves in cheesecloth and tie; add to vinegar mixture. Bring to boiling point. Add vegetables and simmer slowly until vegetables are tender, about ½ hour. Remove cloves. Pack into hot clean jars and seal at once.

Good with beans and corn bread next winter.

DIXIE RELISH

1 gal. ripe tomatoes
12 medium red hot peppers
2½ qt. vinegar
1 Tbsp. celery seed
½ c. salt (not iodized)
1 gal. ground cabbage

1 qt. ground onions
3 lb. brown sugar
4 Tbsp. ground mustard
1 Tbsp. ground cinnamon
2 tsp. turmeric

Grind cabbage; mix with salt. Let stand 2 hours or overnight. Peel onions and grind. Core, quarter, and grind tomatoes and peppers. Mix spice in a little vinegar. With hands, squeeze cabbage out of brine, making it as dry as possible. Throw away brine. Mix all ingredients together. Cook in large enamel container until well done and not too soupy. Pour into hot clean jars and seal at once. Makes 16 pints or there about.

LIME SWEET PICKLES

7 lb. cucumbers, cut into ¼ inch
    pieces
2 c. slack lime (purchase fresh each
    year)
2 gal. water
2 qt. vinegar

1 tsp. celery salt
4½ lb. white sugar
1 Tbsp. mixed pickle spices
1 tsp. whole cloves
1 Tbsp. salt

Soak cucumbers in slack lime and water for 24 hours. Rinse well and cover with cold water; soak 3 hours. Drain well. Cover with the following mixture: Vinegar, celery salt, sugar, pickle spices, cloves, and salt, boiling hot. Soak overnight in mixture.

In the morning, put on stove and let simmer for 35 minutes. Put into hot clean jars and seal at once. May add red or green food coloring before simmering if desired.

ROCHESTER RELISH

½ peck ripe tomatoes (4 qt. equals
    ½ peck)
12 sweet peppers (½ red, ½ green)
6 c. brown sugar
1 tsp. mustard seed
1 Tbsp. cinnamon stick, broken
1 Tbsp. allspice
½ peck green tomatoes

12 small onions
3 stalks celery (or can use
    cabbage)
2 qt. vinegar
1 Tbsp. cloves
½ tsp. mace
1 c. salt

Chop tomatoes, peppers, onions, and celery (or cabbage) coarsely. Add salt and allow to stand overnight; drain. Heat vinegar to boiling. Add sugar. Add spices in a bag. Add chopped vegetables to boiling vinegar. Stir until well blended. Simmer ½ hour. Pour into fruit jars while hot and seal.

Real good next winter with beans and corn bread.

LOST IN THE CEDAR BREAKS

In March 1936 when I was 18 months old, I got lost in the rough breaks 7 miles northwest of Turkey, Texas, toward Mule Creek. My dad had a place leased and it was called the Smith Camp. Mother went out to gather the eggs about 4:00 p.m. and I must have gone out after she did, only I took off the other way. I had a light weight coat on and the weather was cold and windy. When mother got back to the house, she asked my brothers, Red and Frank, where I was, and they didn't know I was gone. She went to the barn and Clyde and Daddy said I wasn't down there. No one had seen me, so they all really started looking for me. They went to a neighbor's, Mrs. Bolton, and I hadn't been there.

Word was passed around that a little girl was lost and over 400 people showed up to look for me. We had about 20 head of horses and they rode all of them. Some went on foot and others used vehicles or anything they could to get around. They used flash lights, lanterns, and vehicle lights. I was found around 8:00 a.m. the next morning. People had looked for me for about 16 hours. I was found at the bottom of a 105 foot bluff, so steep you could hardly climb it. The last 5 feet was straight up and down. I was hung up in some rocks and was cold and blue, but had no broken bones.

Two fellows thought they heard a bobcat and it turned out to be me. I was only 1½ miles from home. They found my dad, and I rode in with him on a paint horse named Tarzan. When Mother and Aunt Annie saw Daddy coming in with me, they jumped the fence and came running to get me. It was really rough country. When I was found, they blew horns and yelled, "She's alive! She's alive!"

Sue, edited by Jean

Notes

Notes

INDEX OF RECIPES

114

MISCELLANEOUS

This Cookbook is a perfect gift for Holidays, Weddings, Anniversaries & Birthdays.

To order extra copies as gifts for your friends, please use Order Forms on reverse side of this page.

* * * * * * * * * *

ORDER FORM

Use the order forms below for obtaining
additional copies of this cookbook.

Fill in Order Forms Below - Cut Out and Mail

You may order as many copies of our Cookbook as you wish for the regular price,
plus $2.00 postage and packing per book ordered. Mail to:

Sue Cunningham   OR   **Jean Cates**
P.O. Box 22, 9th & Smith ⎯   **204 S. Houston**
Hartley, TX 79044   **Amarillo, TX 79102**

Please mail _____ copies of your Cookbook @ _____ each, plus $2.00
postage and packing per book ordered.

Mail books to:

Name _____

Address _____

City, State, Zip _____

You may order as many copies of our Cookbook as you wish for the regular price,
plus $2.00 postage and packing per book ordered. Mail to:

Sue Cunningham   OR   **Jean Cates**
P.O. Box 22, 9th & Smith ⎯   **204 S. Houston**
Hartley, TX 79044   **Amarillo, TX 79102**

Please mail _____ copies of your Cookbook @ _____ each, plus $2.00
postage and packing per book ordered.

Mail books to:

Name _____

Address _____

City, State, Zip _____

1615-94

COOK UP A FUNDRAISING SUCCESS!

You Collect the Recipes *and* We do the Rest!

We have helped thousands of groups like yours,
so let us show you how easy it is to create a successful cookbook.

The following features are included in your cookbook at no additional charge:

* **Washable Full-Color Covers**

* **Seven Full-Color Divider Pages**

* **Professional Typesetting** of recipe pages— not typewritten

* **Three Pages to Print Information** about your organization

* **Table of Contents & Alphabetized Recipe Index**

* **Coupon Page** to help you sell your cookbooks

* **Colorful Full Length Plastic Ring Binders** allowing book to lie flat while in use

* **We Pay the Freight with FREE Cookbooks** on every order

Send Coupon below or Call TOLL-FREE 1-800-227-7282

COOKBOOK PUBLISHERS, INC.®
"Quality is our Main Ingredient"

10800 Lakeview Ave.
P.O. Box 15920
Lenexa, Kansas 66285-5920

Yes, Please rush the FREE — No Obligation details on how my group can use your easy fundraising plan.

No. of Members

Organization _____

Name _____

Address _____

City _____ State _____ Zip _____

Home Phone _____ Work Phone _____

CP-988

We Can Create a Cookbook For You Too!

It's Fun — It's Easy — It's Profitable

All you have to do is furnish recipes and we provide FREE recipe forms to help you. Your book is completely personalized because your organization's name and town are printed on the front cover. The name of every person who submits a recipe is printed right with their recipes.

Your Books Are Self Financing

You figure the cost of your books from our Price Chart. Costs are based on the number of recipes you want printed and the number of books you want to order.

NO DOWN PAYMENT
NO INTEREST OR HANDLING CHARGES

One-half of balance 37 days after books are shipped—remaining balance, 67 days after books are shipped. Thirty-day extension on written request if needed (making a total of 97 days).

For Your FREE Step-by-Step Instruction Kit simply RETURN the POSTAGE PAID CARD NOW or CALL TOLL FREE!
1-800-227-7282

(Tear along perforation, fill in reverse side and mail)

NO POSTAGE
NECESSARY
IF MAILED
IN THE
UNITED STATES

BUSINESS REPLY MAIL

FIRST-CLASS MAIL PERMIT NO. 4483 SHAWNEE MISSION KS

POSTAGE WILL BE PAID BY ADDRESSEE

COOKBOOK PUBLISHERS INC
10800 LAKEVIEW AVE
PO BOX 15920
LENEXA KS 66285-9802

SAVORY POT ROAST

Prep Time: 5 min.   Cook Time: 3 hr.

2 tbsp. vegetable oil
3½ to 4 lb. beef round or chuck pot roast
1 can (10¾ oz.) CAMPBELL'S® Cream of Mushroom Soup
1 pouch CAMPBELL'S® Dry Onion Quality Soup and Recipe Mix

1¼ cups water
6 medium potatoes, quartered
6 carrots, cut into 2" pieces
2 tbsp. all-purpose flour

1. In 6-qt. Dutch oven, in hot oil, brown roast. Spoon off fat.

2. Add mushroom soup, onion soup mix and 1 cup water. Cover; cook over low heat 2 hr. Add vegetables. Cover; cook 45 min. or until roast and vegetables are fork-tender, stirring occasionally.

3. Remove roast and vegetables. Stir together flour and remaining ¼ cup water until smooth. Gradually stir into soup mixture. Cook until mixture boils and thickens, stirring constantly. 8 servings.

SAVE 10¢

When You Buy Any Size Louisiana Hot Sauce Product

Consumer: This coupon good only on product indicated. Limit one coupon per purchase. Void if copied or reproduced. Retailer: You are authorized to redeem this coupon at face value plus 8¢ handling where the terms of the offer have been complied with in accordance with our redemption policy (copy available upon request). Retailers and authorized clearing houses, send coupons to: Bruce Foods Corporation, CMS Dept. #17600, One Faucett Drive, Del Rio, TX 78840.

1024

5 17600 21010 9

SAVE 50¢

When You Buy Any Size Casa Fiesta Salsa, Taco or Picante Sauce

Consumer: This coupon good only on product indicated. Limit one coupon per purchase. Void if copied or reproduced. Retailer: You are authorized to redeem this coupon at face value plus 8¢ handling where the terms of the offer have been complied with in accordance with our redemption policy (copy available upon request). Retailers and authorized clearing houses, send coupons to: Bruce Foods Corporation, CMS Dept. #17600, One Faucett Drive, Del Rio, TX 78840.

1025

5 17600 80050 3

SAVE 25¢

When You Buy Any Size Casa Fiesta Taco Shell, Taco Tray or Taco Dinner

Consumer: This coupon good only on product indicated. Limit one coupon per purchase. Void if copied or reproduced. Retailer: You are authorized to redeem this coupon at face value plus 8¢ handling where the terms of the offer have been complied with in accordance with our redemption policy (copy available upon request). Retailers and authorized clearing houses, send coupons to: Bruce Foods Corporation, CMS Dept. #17600, One Faucett Drive, Del Rio, TX 78840.

1026

5 17600 80025 6

SAVE 15¢

When You Buy Any Size Casa Fiesta Seasoning Mix or Bean Product

Consumer: This coupon good only on product indicated. Limit one coupon per purchase. Void if copied or reproduced. Retailer: You are authorized to redeem this coupon at face value plus 8¢ handling where the terms of the offer have been complied with in accordance with our redemption policy (copy available upon request). Retailers and authorized clearing houses, send coupons to: Bruce Foods Corporation, CMS Dept. #17600, One Faucett Drive, Del Rio, TX 78840.

1027

5 17600 80015 7